David Copperfield

CHARLES DICKENS

Level 3

Retold by Nigel Grimshaw
Series Editors: Andy Hopkins and Jocelyn Potter

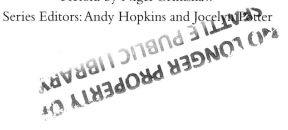

Pearson Education Limited
Edinburgh Gate, Harlow,
Essex CM20 2JE, England
and Associated Companies throughout the world.

ISBN: 978-1-4058-6240-0

First published in the Longman Structural Readers Series 1968
This adaptation first published by Addison Wesley Longman Limited
in the Longman Fiction Series 1996
First published by Penguin Books 1999
This edition published 2008

9 10

Text copyright © Penguin Books Ltd 1999
This edition copyright © Pearson Education Ltd 2008
Illustrations by John Lawrence

Typeset by Graphicraft Ltd, Hong Kong
Set in 11/14pt Bembo
Printed in China
SWTC/09

Published by Pearson Education Ltd in association with
Penguin Books Ltd, both companies being subsidiaries of Pearson Plc

For a complete list of the titles available in the Penguin Readers series please write to your local
Pearson Longman office or to: Penguin Readers Marketing Department, Pearson Education,
Edinburgh Gate, Harlow, Essex CM20 2JE, England.

Contents

Introduction

Miss Trotwood sat in a chair and waited. When the doctor came downstairs again, she jumped up.

'Has the baby arrived?' she asked.

'Yes,' he said.

'And how is she?'

'She is a he,' he told her. 'The baby is a boy.'

Without a word, Miss Trotwood picked up her hat and left the house. She never saw my mother again.

The baby's name is David Copperfield. He has only been alive for a few minutes but already somebody dislikes him! At first, there seems to be no other problems. David grows up in a loving home with his mother and her servant and friend, Peggotty. But there are other people in the world, and David's problems soon begin. His mother falls in love with a man called Mr Murdstone. Mr Murdstone does not like David and is cruel to him. David is sent away to a terrible school where he finds more cruelty. There are times of hope and happiness. He enjoys his visits to Yarmouth, by the sea, staying with Peggotty's brother. But David's life is never going to be easy...

As we follow David on his journey through life, we meet many interesting people. Some of them are good people and some of them are bad. Some are the most unforgettable people in English literature. Mr Micawber is a man who always owes money. Uriah Heep is a 'very humble' man who brings pain and sadness to everyone around him. Steerforth is David's best friend – but what is his secret? Then there are the women – beautiful but childlike Dora, sweet Agnes Wickfield ... and many more.

Will David ever find happiness in a world where cruel people are strong and good people are often weak? Read his story and find out!

Charles Dickens began writing *David Copperfield* in 1849, when he was thirty-seven years old. He was already famous for many earlier stories – *The Pickwick Papers* (1837), *Oliver Twist* (1838), *Nicholas Nickleby* (1839), *The Old Curosity Shop* (1841) and *A Christmas Carol* (1843) – and *David Copperfield* was an immediate success.

Dickens's stories are often about children with no parents (*Oliver Twist*) or with only one parent (*Nicholas Nickleby, David Copperfield*). In a hard world, strong – often rich – people are cruel to these children. David Copperfield, like other poor children in Dickens's stories, is a good person, but he suffers terribly. He is badly hurt in love, he is hated by his new father, and even his best friend is dishonest with him. There are other good people in the story, too, but they also suffer. Dickens's story shows that weak people need the help of strong, good people. Without this help, they cannot win the fight against people who are strong and cruel. In *Nicholas Nickleby*, Nicholas succeeds with the help of the rich Cheeryble brothers; in *Oliver Twist*, Oliver gets the help of Mr Brownlowe; in *David Copperfield*, David has to ask for the help of Miss Betsey Trotwood. She is the woman who refused to help his mother after his birth.

Dickens's books gave a true picture of the hard life that poor children suffered in those days. They also showed people the importance of good friends and families. Most importantly, perhaps, they showed readers that things had to change. Sometimes, as a result of Dickens's work, they did. After *Nicholas Nickleby*, for example, the government shut many bad schools in the north of England.

David Copperfield, of course, is not just about the unfairness of life and the seriousness of its problems. It is also a story about everyone's search for happiness. It is an exciting adventure story and is often very amusing. It is as popular today as it was in the 1840s, and there have been many films of the story.

Charles Dickens was born in Portsmouth, England, in 1812. He was the eldest son in a family of eight children. His father was a clerk, but went to prison in 1824 because he owed money. Twelve-year-old Charles had to work cleaning shoes and in a bottle factory, but he always dreamt of better things. In 1827, he worked as a clerk in a law company, but he hated the law and soon left. He was interested in acting, but decided to work in the newspaper business. In 1832, he became a reporter and his first story, *A Dinner at Poplar Walk*, came out in *The Monthly Magazine*.

In 1836, Dickens married Catherine Hogarth, the daughter of an important man at *The Evening Chronicle* newspaper. A year later, he and Catherine had the first of their ten children, and his first book, *The Pickwick Papers*, came out in monthly parts. When the last part came out in November 1837, his story had 40,000 readers! His next books, *Oliver Twist* and *Nicholas Nickleby*, made him famous. *David Copperfield* was followed by many more books and stories. The most famous of these, perhaps, are *A Tale of Two Cities* (1859) and *Great Expectations* (1861).

Dickens never lost his love of the theatre. In 1857 he acted in *The Frozen Deep*, a play by his friend, Wilkie Collins. While he was acting in this play, he fell in love with an actress, Ellen Teman. He left his wife a year later.

He also became famous in the United States, and he went on two reading tours there. During his second visit in 1867, he was very ill but he refused to stop working. He died in June, 1870, leaving an unfinished book, *The Mystery of Edwin Drood*. He was only fifty-eight years old, but he was already one of the greatest writers in the history of English literature.

Chapter 1   I Have a New Father

It was a terrible stormy night six months after my father's death. My mother was sitting alone by the fire, waiting for her baby to arrive. She was feeling sad and ill. Suddenly she heard a noise outside.

'There's someone at the door, Peggotty,' my mother called. 'Who is it?' Peggotty was her servant and her only real friend.

'I'll go and see,' Peggotty replied. She went and opened the door. Miss Trotwood, my father's aunt, followed Peggotty into the sitting room. This was her first visit since my parents' marriage, because she did not have a high opinion of my mother.

'Where's the baby?' she asked. Her loud voice frightened my mother, who began to cry.

'It isn't here yet,' my mother said unhappily. 'It will come soon.'

'Dear, dear,' Miss Trotwood said in her loud voice. 'You're only a baby yourself, aren't you? Now your husband is dead and you're alone. But don't worry. The baby will be a little girl and I like little girls. You can call her Betsey Trotwood Copperfield. Then I'll help you look after the baby.'

'Thank you,' my mother said. 'I'm sorry. I have to leave you now. I don't feel well. I'm going to my room.' She called Peggotty, who took her slowly upstairs. Soon after that the doctor arrived. Miss Trotwood sat in a chair and waited. When the doctor came downstairs again, she jumped up.

'Has the baby arrived?' she asked.

'Yes,' he said.

'And how is she?'

'She is a he,' he told her. 'The baby is a boy.'

Without a word, Miss Trotwood picked up her hat and left the house. She never saw my mother again.

Miss Trotwood, my father's aunt, followed Peggotty into the sitting room.

◆

I was that baby and my name is David Copperfield. The years went past and I reached the age of six. At that time I knew two people – my mother and Peggotty. I loved them very much and Peggotty was always good and kind. We were all very happy together.

My mother and I went to church every Sunday. One Sunday a man stopped us when we were leaving the church. He had black hair and dark eyes and I was afraid of him.

'Good morning, Mrs Copperfield,' he said.

'Good morning, Mr Murdstone,' she answered.

'I hope that you are well,' he continued. He was smiling at me in a way that I did not like. I did not smile.

'Very well, thank you, Mr Murdstone,' she said.

He put his hand on my head. 'Is this David, your little boy?' he asked. I moved quickly away. He looked angry for a moment. Then he smiled at my mother. 'May I call at your house?' he asked.

'Please do,' she said. He said goodbye and left us.

I did not want to see him again, but after that he often came to the house. My mother liked him but Peggotty did not. One day I found them both in tears.

'He's not like Mr Copperfield,' Peggotty was saying.

'Why do you make me feel so uncomfortable?' my mother replied. 'My husband is dead and I have no friends here. I am doing nothing wrong.'

Mr Murdstone took me to Lowestoft. I did not like him at all but I wanted to go there. It is a nice town by the sea. We met some friends of Mr Murdstone.

'Your friend, Mrs Copperfield, is very pretty, isn't she?' one man said.

'Be quiet! This boy understands things and he'll tell his

mother,' said Mr Murdstone. They all laughed.

Later I told my mother about the conversation.

'Don't say that. It isn't true.' Her face was red but she was laughing.

Some months went past. One day my mother asked, 'David, do you like the sea?'

'Oh, yes!' I said.

'You can have a holiday by the sea,' she said.

'Where shall we go?' I asked.

'Not "we" David,' she said. 'I won't be with you. You can go with Peggotty to Yarmouth. Her brother lives there and you can stay with him. Will you like that?'

'Oh, yes!' I said again. 'Very much! Why aren't you coming, too?'

'I can't tell you now,' she said. 'When you come back, you'll understand.'

So Peggotty and I went to Yarmouth. Mr Peggotty's house was a boat on the beach with a door and windows in the side and I liked it very much. There was a strong smell of fish but everything was very clean. Four people lived in the house. Ham lived there with his uncle, Mr Peggotty, because his father was dead. Little Emily was the daughter of another sister of Mr Peggotty and both her parents were dead. The fourth person was Mrs Gummidge. Like Mr Peggotty's brother and his sister's husband, Mr Gummidge was a fisherman and died at sea. Mr Peggotty was a fisherman too. He was a very kind man and loved his unusual family.

Little Emily was a beautiful child. As soon as I saw her, I fell in love with her. At first she was rather frightened of me, but we became friends. We often went down to the sea together. We sat on the sand and looked at the water.

'I'm afraid of it,' Emily said. 'Are you afraid of the sea?'

'No,' I said. But this was not quite true.

'The sea killed my father,' she said.

'I know,' I said.

'When my father died, Mr Peggotty looked after me. He's a good man,' she told me.

'Yes, he is,' I agreed. 'He's very kind. I like him very much.'

'When I'm a lady, I'll have a lot of money,' Emily said. 'Then I'll buy nice clothes and a big gold watch for Mr Peggotty and give him a box of money.'

'Would you like to be a lady then?' I asked.

'Yes,' she explained. 'Then the stormy weather won't hurt us, and we can help the poor fishermen. They can't work if they have an accident.'

Mrs Gummidge was not sweet and loving like Emily. She was always unhappy and she complained a lot. When Mr Peggotty went out, Mrs Gummidge complained about that.

'Where's Mr Peggotty?' she asked. 'He's left me alone. He doesn't think about my feelings. Nobody thinks about my feelings.'

This was not true. Mr Peggotty looked after Mrs Gummidge very well. He let her live in his house and was always kind to her. He never got angry when she complained.

I enjoyed my time in Yarmouth, but it soon ended. I was very sorry to leave. I did not want to leave my new friends. I was very sad to leave little Emily.

'Goodbye, Emily,' I said. 'I don't want to leave here.'

'Goodbye, David,' she said. 'I shall miss you.'

'I'll miss you, too,' I told her. 'I'll write to you.'

'Please do that,' she answered. 'And don't forget me.'

When I saw our house again, I felt happier.

'We're home, Peggotty!' I cried. 'Won't Mother be pleased?' But Peggotty did not answer.

A new servant opened the door. She told us that my mother was not at home.

'Where's Mother?' I asked Peggotty. 'Why isn't she here to meet us?'

'Wait,' Peggotty said. 'She'll explain.'

'No!' I said. '*You* tell me, now. Where is she?' I suddenly felt frightened. 'Is she dead like my father?'

'Oh, no!' said Peggotty, taking me in her arms. 'She isn't dead.'

'What's wrong?' I cried. 'Where is she?'

'I'll tell you,' said Peggotty. She wasn't looking at me now. 'You have a new father. What do you think about that?'

'Who is he?' I asked. 'Is he . . . ?'

'Yes,' Peggotty said. 'Your new father is Mr Murdstone. Your mother is Mrs Murdstone now.'

Chapter 2   I Am Sent Away from Home

I went to my bedroom. I hid my face in the sheets and I cried. At that moment my mother came home and found me there.

'Davy, Davy, my child. What's the matter?' she asked, and she went down on her knees next to the bed.

'What's this? Clara, my love, have you forgotten?' It was Mr Murdstone's voice from the door. 'Don't be soft with the child. He has to learn to be a man.' He sent my mother downstairs and pulled the sheets away from me. 'David,' he said, with his thin lips. 'If a horse or a dog is bad, what do we do to them?'

'I don't know.'

'We beat them. Do you understand me? Right. Now stop that noise and wash your face.'

Mr Murdstone's sister came to stay with us. She was dark like her brother, with a hard face and a large nose. She walked through the house and she looked at all the rooms. She found dirt in all of them. On that first morning she said, 'Clara, I'll manage the house.'

My mother did not like this but said nothing. Time passed, though, and she had nothing at all to do. Miss Murdstone was making changes without even asking her. My mother made the mistake of complaining to her new husband.

'Don't be silly,' Mr Murdstone said. 'You can't manage the house, Clara. You should be grateful that my sister has more good sense.'

'I'll go,' said Miss Murdstone, when she heard about this conversation. 'I'll leave the house *now*!'

'No,' said Mr Murdstone. 'Clara is being silly. I want you to stay. We need you here.'

My mother cried but she did not complain again.

Before her marriage my mother taught me my lessons, but now Mr Murdstone became my teacher. Because I was frightened of him, I could not learn anything. He got very angry.

'This boy is stupid and lazy,' he said to my mother day after day. 'He refuses to learn, so he won't have any dinner today.' I was usually given only a piece of bread in my room.

Then, one day, Mr Murdstone brought a stick with him.

'Remember your lessons or I'll hit you,' he said.

I tried hard to learn, but I could not.

'You're a bad, stupid boy! Come with me!' he ordered, pulling me to my room.

'Please, Mr Murdstone!' I said. '*Please* don't hit me! I can't learn from you. I want to learn and I try to learn. But I can't!'

'You *can* learn and you *will* learn!' he said. He held my head under his arm and he hit me very hard. I shouted with the pain. Then I bit his hand!

He was very angry. He beat me until I fell to the floor. After that, he left the room. He turned the key in the door and took it with him.

The house was quiet. I could not hear anything at all. My

mother did not come to my room, and I felt quite alone.

The morning passed; the afternoon passed; the evening passed. Night came and my door stayed locked. Then I heard the sound of footsteps on the stairs. The key turned and Miss Murdstone came into the room. She gave me some food but she did not speak to me. The next day she came again.

'You can walk in the garden,' she said. So I went for a walk.

The next five days were like this. I did not see my mother. I saw only Miss Murdstone. She had the key, and I could not leave my room without permission. Then one night Peggotty came. The door was locked and she spoke through it.

'Peggotty,' I said, 'is that you?'

'Yes, David,' she replied. She was crying and I was crying, too.

'Is my mother angry with me?' I asked.

'No, she isn't angry,' Peggotty said.

'What is Mr Murdstone going to do to me?' I asked.

'You're going to go to a school,' Peggotty said. 'It's near London.'

'When do I have to go?'

'Tomorrow morning,' Peggotty said. 'Don't forget me. I won't forget you. I'll look after your mother.'

'Thank you, dear Peggotty!' I said. 'Promise me one thing. Write to Mr Peggotty and Emily. I am not a bad boy. Tell them that.'

'I will, David,' Peggotty said. 'I'll write to them tomorrow, I promise.'

The next morning Miss Murdstone came and put my clothes in a box. She sent me downstairs to have breakfast with my mother.

'Oh, David,' my mother said. She looked sad and pale, and her eyes were red. 'You've hurt Mr Murdstone and you've hurt me. I forgive you, but try to be better.'

I could not eat; my tears fell on my bread and butter. My

He held my head under his arm and he hit me very hard.

mother looked at me and then at Miss Murdstone. She said nothing.

We heard the wheels outside the gate and my box was lifted into the cart.

'Goodbye, David,' said my mother. 'You're going for your own good. You will come home for the holidays and be a better boy.'

'Clara!' ordered Miss Murdstone. 'Let the boy go.' She took me to the cart. I got in and we drove away.

Chapter 3 I Start School at Salem House

The cart took me to Yarmouth. Mr Barkis, the driver, asked me a lot of questions about Peggotty. He wanted to marry her but he was afraid to speak to her about it.

From Yarmouth I took a coach to London. The coach was full of people and we drove all night. I felt cold and uncomfortable. I was excited, though, when we reached London. Everyone got out and I was left alone. I sat down and waited. At last a young man arrived. He was very thin and he wore dark, rather dirty clothes.

'Are you the new boy?' he asked.

'Yes, sir,' I said.

'Come with me,' he said. 'My name's Mell. I teach at Salem House. I'll take you there. It's on the other side of London, about six miles from here.'

'Can I buy some food?' I asked. 'I had nothing on the journey, and I'm very hungry.'

'Yes,' he said. 'We'll go to my mother's house and you can eat it there.'

So I bought some bread and some eggs and we went to a small house near London Bridge. It was clear that his mother was very poor. When she saw her son, her eyes lit up. I sat down near the small fire while she cooked the eggs. I ate them with great enjoyment.

'Play your pipe,' Mrs Mell said. Her son took his pipe from his pocket and played a song on it. He played badly but his mother smiled happily. Then we left her poor little house and went to the school. There was nobody there. It was, I thought, probably the school holidays.

'This is your new home,' Mr Mell told me. 'Follow me.' He took me to the schoolroom, a big, empty place. On one desk there was a large board. On it was written: 'Stay away. He bites!'

'Please, Mr Mell,' I said. 'Where's the dog?'

'What dog?' he asked. I showed him the board. 'There isn't a dog,' he told me. 'That board is for you. I'm sorry about this, but I have my orders. You have to wear it.'

That night I slept at the school. When I got up, Mr Mell tied the board to my back. I had to wear it every day and I suffered terribly.

I was alone in the school, so I walked around it. On an old door in the playground were a lot of names. Two of the names that interested me were "Steerforth" and "Traddles". I often thought about those two boys.

Mr Creakle, the owner of the school, came back one day. That night Mr Mell took me to see him. He had an angry red face and small eyes deep in his head. He spoke very softly, which made him sound even angrier. I was afraid of his soft voice and I was afraid of him.

He held my ear. 'Listen to me,' he said. 'I'm a hard man and I don't like bad boys. So be good.'

'Yes, sir,' I said, 'I will. Please, sir?'

'What?' he asked in an angry voice.

'I don't want to wear this board when the other boys return,' I said.

'What?' Mr Creakle cried. 'You have to wear it every day. Now go!' He stood up with such a terrible look on his face that I ran from the room.

Traddles came back to the school first. He turned my board into a joke. I liked him very much.

The other boys were not so kind. 'Look at that boy!' they said. 'Look at that board on his back. He bites like a dog.'

When they laughed at me I felt unhappy and alone.

Finally Steerforth arrived. He was about six years older than me, clever and very good-looking.

'Hello, Copperfield,' he said. He asked about my punishment on the first day, but never talked about it again. I was pleased about that. 'Have you any money?' he asked.

'Yes,' I said. 'Seven shillings.'

'Give it to me,' he said. 'I'll manage it for you.' I gave him the money. 'You want to spend some, don't you?' he said.

'I don't know,' I told him.

'Yes, you do,' he said. 'I'll buy some wine and cakes with it.'

That seemed to me to be a good idea. That night we ate the cakes and drank the wine in our bedroom. All the boys slept in one room. They told me about the school. Mr Creakle was a cruel, unpopular man and he was a bad teacher.

The next day Mr Creakle visited our classroom. He was carrying a stick and he came straight to my desk.

'Copperfield!' he said. 'You bite, don't you? So do I.' He showed me the stick. 'This is my bite,' he said and he hit me hard. 'Do you like it?' he asked and he hit me again. 'Is it nice?' Again he hit me and I cried.

We did not like that first day of lessons. Mr Creakle beat all the boys but for some reason he did not touch Steerforth.

The weeks passed. Every night I told Steerforth a long story. He enjoyed the stories and he became my friend. Mr Mell liked me, too. He taught me and I learned my lessons well. After a time he took my board away.

'Look at that board on his back. He bites like a dog.'

One day we had a holiday, so we did not have to do any work. We were all in the schoolroom with Mr Mell, playing noisily. Steerforth was the noisiest of all of us.

'Steerforth!' Mr Mell said. 'Be quiet!'

'Who are *you* talking to?' Steerforth said.

'I'm talking to you, Steerforth,' Mr Mell said. 'Don't be so rude.'

'I'm not rude,' Steerforth said. 'I'm a gentleman, and you're only a poor teacher. A gentleman can't be rude to a poor man.'

'You're not a gentleman,' Mr Mell said.

'Be quiet!' Steerforth cried. 'Be quiet or I'll hit you!'

'What's the matter here?' Mr Creakle came into the room. He looked very angry. 'Mr Mell,' he said. 'What are you doing?'

'Steerforth was rude to me,' Mr Mell said.

'Steerforth?' Mr Creakle asked. 'But his mother's a very rich woman and he's a gentleman. Were you rude, Steerforth?'

'No,' Steerforth said. 'I just said that he was poor. I know that his mother is very poor, too.'

'Is this true?' Mr Creakle asked Mr Mell.

'Yes,' Mr Mell said. 'You knew my position when I came here.'

'I think that you are probably in the wrong job, Mr Mell,' said Mr Creakle. 'All the teachers here are gentlemen. We don't want poor men here.'

'I'll leave,' said Mr Mell.

'Yes,' said Mr Creakle. 'Please leave now.'

We all watched Mr Mell. He took his pipe and his books from the desk and he left the room. We were all quiet and we did not look at Steerforth.

Later, Traddles said, 'I'm sorry that Mr Mell has gone.'

'Sorry?' said Steerforth. 'Why are you sorry? That's stupid.'

'Mr Mell's poor and now he hasn't any work. He needs to earn money for his mother,' Traddles said.

'I'll send him money,' Steerforth said. 'I'm rich. But he was rude to me and I don't like rude men.'

I was sorry, too. I liked Steerforth, but Mr Mell was always kind to me, too. He helped me with my lessons and I enjoyed learning from him. We never saw him again.

◆

One happy day Mr Peggotty and Ham came to see me.

'Hello, David,' said Mr Peggotty. 'We're visiting London because we have some work here. We wanted to see you and so we asked my sister for your address.'

'It's so nice to see you,' I said. 'How is little Emily?'

'Well,' said Mr Peggotty. 'She's very well. She's becoming a woman now. Ask him!' He meant Ham, who agreed happily.

'And Mrs Gummidge?' I asked.

'She's very well, thank you,' he said.

'We've brought you a present,' Ham said. 'Do you like fish?'

'Oh, yes,' I said. 'Very much.' I did. I was always hungry at school.

Suddenly Steerforth came into the room. When he saw Ham and Mr Peggotty he stopped. 'I'm very sorry,' he said. 'I didn't know that you were here. I'm interrupting you.'

'You're not interrupting us,' I said. 'Meet my friends. This is Mr Peggotty and this is Ham.' Steerforth shook hands with each of them. 'Mr Peggotty has a house in Yarmouth,' I continued. 'It's made from an old boat.'

'That's very interesting,' Steerforth said. 'It sounds like the right kind of house for a boatman.'

'If I come to Yarmouth,' I said, 'can I bring Steerforth? He's so kind to me. We can visit your house together.'

'Yes,' said Mr Peggotty. 'It's not a very fine house, but we'll be happy to have you. Don't forget.'

He and Ham left then. That night we ate the fish and it was excellent.

At last the happiest day arrived – the first day of the holidays. I was very pleased to leave the school.

Chapter 4   I Grow Up

I took the coach to Yarmouth, where Barkis was waiting to drive me home. When we got there my mother was singing softly. I heard her voice first and then she came to the door. She had a new baby in her arms.

She put her arms round me and kissed me. Peggotty was very happy to see me, too.

We ate by the fire and Peggotty ate with us. I told her that Barkis wanted to marry her. She laughed but her face went red. She could not look at us and she put her hands over her face. 'Barkis is being silly,' she said.

'Oh!' my mother said sadly. 'Will you marry Barkis? Will you leave me, Peggotty?'

'No,' Peggotty said. 'I won't leave you, my love. I'll stay here until I'm old and useless. Then I'll go to David and ask him to look after me.' She put her arms round my mother and we all sat quietly together.

Then we talked a little about Mr Murdstone. Peggotty did not like him at all. 'He's not kind to David,' she said.

'Yes, he is,' my mother said. 'He does his best. He's my husband, Peggotty, and you're making me angry.'

'Don't be angry,' Peggotty said. 'I'm sorry.'

'I'm not really angry,' said my mother. 'I'm very happy that David has come home. Will you read us a story, David?'

I read them a story and we were very happy and comfortable together. Then, at about ten o'clock, we heard people outside. Mr Murdstone and his sister were returning home.

'Go to bed now, David,' said my mother in a low voice.

'Go quickly.'

I went to bed and I did not see Mr Murdstone that night.

I did see him the next morning. He was standing near the fire in the sitting room and I went to him. 'I'm very sorry that I bit you, sir,' I said. He shook my hand but he did not speak. His eyes were as cold and cruel as I remembered them.

Miss Murdstone was sitting at the table. 'How long are the holidays?' she asked. 'When do you go back to school?'

'In a month,' I replied.

'A month! That's a long time.' She thought for a moment. Then she looked happier.

'But one day has already gone,' she said. 'You'll soon leave us again.'

Mr Murdstone did not often speak to me. Usually I sat with my mother and Miss Murdstone. My little brother was always with us. I loved him very much. One day when my mother was holding the baby, I took him from her.

'Clara!' cried Miss Murdstone.

'What is it?' asked my mother.

'Don't let that boy hold the baby!' Miss Murdstone cried. 'He'll hurt it!' She quickly took the baby from me. I felt hurt and unhappy.

When I was with Mr Murdstone and his sister, I was very uncomfortable. So I stayed in my room and read stories. I often sat in Peggotty's room, too, and talked to her. Mr Murdstone did not like this and one day he sent for me.

'David,' he said. 'You are being very rude. Every day you stay in your room or you sit with uneducated servants.' He meant Peggotty. 'You should spend time with me and my sister. You will come into the sitting room every night and sit with your mother, Miss Murdstone and me.'

Every night I sat with them, but they never spoke to me. Mr Murdstone and his sister had nothing to say and my mother was afraid of making them angry. I read schoolbooks until nine o'clock and then I went to bed. I did this every night. Then the holidays finished and Barkis came with his cart.

I said goodbye to Mr Murdstone and to Miss Murdstone and I kissed my mother. Then I left the house. My mother stood at the door watching me. She held up the baby and smiled. Then the cart turned the corner. I did not see either of them again.

◆

Two months passed. One day Mrs Creakle sent for me. I went to the rooms where she lived with Mr Creakle. 'David,' she said, and her voice was very kind. 'Be strong. I'm afraid I have some bad news for you. Your mother is very ill.'

I did not speak. I waited.

'She is dangerously ill,' she added. The tears started to run down my cheeks. I knew now.

'Your mother is dead,' she told me.

'And my little brother–?' I asked.

'He is very ill,' she said. 'He is very, very ill. You can go home tomorrow.'

I cried all day, and she kept me with her. Then the next day I said goodbye to the other boys and travelled home. I did not know that I was never going to return.

◆

I saw Miss Murdstone first. She did not say, 'I'm sorry about your mother's death.' She spoke coldly.

'Go to your room and go quickly,' she said. 'I hope that you've brought your good shirts with you.'

Mr Murdstone did not speak to me at all. He walked around the house crying quietly. He carried a book but he could not read it. My little brother was dead too, and he was very sad.

Peggotty put her arms round me.

'Your mother's illness began a long time ago,' she told me. 'She talked about you every day. She loved you very much. Remember her always.'

'I will! Oh, I will!' I said. But I wanted to remember her as she was before her marriage to Mr Murdstone. It was only after that that she became unhappy.

I did not go back to school. Schools cost money and Mr Murdstone did not want to spend anything on my education. So I stayed in the sad, uncomfortable house. Now that my mother was dead, both Mr Murdstone and his sister hated me openly.

'Mr Murdstone doesn't want me to stay here,' Peggotty told me while we were sitting in her room one day. 'I have to find new work. I'll go to Yarmouth. Will you come with me? We can have a holiday together.'

The Murdstones let me go to Yarmouth. We made the journey in Barkis's cart. He was very happy to sit with Peggotty and she clearly liked Barkis too. We arrived at Mr Peggotty's house and he was very pleased to see us. The house looked just the same, except perhaps a little smaller. Only little Emily was missing.

'Where's Emily?' I asked.

'She's at school,' Mr Peggotty explained.

'Why doesn't she come?' Mrs Gummidge complained. Mrs Gummidge was the same as ever.

'She'll come soon,' Mr Peggotty said.

When Emily arrived, she was surprised to see us. She was older now and looked very pretty.

'Hello, Emily,' I greeted her. 'Can I kiss you?'

'No,' she said, going red. 'I don't like kissing. It's silly.'

Later she came to me and took my hand. 'I know that your mother and your little brother are dead,' she said. 'I'm very sorry, David.' Her blue eyes were wet with tears. She looked very sad.

We all ate at Mr Peggotty's house. After the meal, we talked together.

'How is your friend, Steerforth?' Mr Peggotty asked. 'He's a very fine boy.'

'Yes, he is,' I agreed. 'He's clever, too. He learns very quickly. He's well, I think.'

'Look at Emily,' said Mr Peggotty and he laughed. 'She hasn't seen Steerforth yet. But she likes him already.'

Emily's face was red. She put her hands over her face and Mr Peggotty and Ham laughed. They loved Emily very much and they gave her everything.

Our visit to Yarmouth was as happy as the last one. One day I had a big surprise. Mr Barkis was also staying in Yarmouth, and Peggotty went out with him for the afternoon. They were both wearing their best clothes. When they came back, they were married. Peggotty was now Mrs Barkis.

But the happy time soon ended and I went home alone. Peggotty had her own little house now, with Mr Barkis. She promised me, though, that I was always welcome there. Mr Murdstone did not hit me and he and his sister gave me food. But they said very little to me.

One day Mr Murdstone sent for me. There was a second man in the room with him.

'This is Mr Quinion, David,' Mr Murdstone said. 'He has a business in London. You will work for him and you will earn enough money to buy your own food. I'll pay for your room. You'll go to London with Mr Quinion tomorrow.'

Chapter 5   I Go to Work

Mr Quinion had a business selling wines to passenger ships. The building was very dark and dirty. Two boys worked with me washing dirty bottles. They were then filled again with wine. At that time I was only ten years old. I hated the work.

'She hasn't seen Steerforth yet. But she likes him already.'

On the first day Mr Quinion sent for me and introduced me to a gentleman in old but cheerful clothes. He did not have a single hair on his head.

'This is Mr Micawber,' said Mr Quinion. 'You'll live with him while you are working here.' We shook hands.

'I am pleased to meet you, Mr Copperfield. When do you finish work?' Mr Micawber asked.

'At eight o'clock, sir,' I said.

'I'll come here then,' Mr Micawber said. 'I'll take you to my house. It's easy to get lost in my part of town.'

That night Mr Micawber took me home. His house was big but there was little furniture in it. Mrs Micawber told me about her husband. 'Mr Micawber has no luck,' she said. 'He isn't lucky with money. He owes money to a lot of people and he can't pay them.'

Every week Mr Quinion paid me six shillings and I spent all the money on food. In the morning I ate a piece of bread and I drank a cup of milk. At night I ate bread again. It was a hard life. I was poor and often very hungry.

But the Micawbers were always poor, too. 'Will you help me, David?' Mrs Micawber asked one day. 'There isn't any money in the house and we haven't any food.'

I put my hand into my pocket without a second thought. 'I have two shillings here,' I told her. 'Please take them.'

'Thank you, David,' she said unhappily. 'But I don't want *your* money. I want to sell Mr Micawber's books. Will you take the books to a shop for me?'

'Of course,' I answered. I sold the books for Mrs Micawber and gave her the money. This made her happy again and she kissed me. After that I often sold things for her. But this money was not enough to pay everyone that Mr Micawber owed. In the end the police came and took the Micawbers to prison. I had to leave their house when everything in it was sold. I found a small room by the prison, though, and I often visited them.

Then Mrs Micawber's family helped the Micawbers with a large sum of money, and my friends were able to leave the prison at last. We all had dinner together.

'Tomorrow we are going to Plymouth,' Mr Micawber told me. 'I have work in Plymouth. I'll begin a new and better life there. But we are leaving you, David, and I'm very sorry about that. Let me teach you a lesson before I go. If you earn twenty pounds a year, you should only spend nineteen pounds nineteen shillings and sixpence. Then you'll be happy. If you spend twenty pounds and one shilling, the result is unhappiness.'

'Thank you,' I said. 'I'll remember that.'

The next day the Micawbers left. I gave presents to their children and Mrs Micawber kissed me warmly. I felt sad and alone again.

'I haven't any friends now,' I thought. 'I hate London.' Then I had an idea. 'I'll leave my job and go to my aunt, Betsey Trotwood,' I thought.

I wrote to Peggotty and I asked her for money for the journey. She sent me a letter with the money and gave me my aunt's address in Dover. 'I'll go to Dover on Saturday,' I thought.

On Saturday I collected my box from my little room. A young man was passing, driving a cart along the road.

'Will you take my box, please?' I asked.

'Where to?' he said.

'To the Dover coach, please.'

He threw my box onto the cart. I did not like the look of the young man, so I hid my money in my mouth. 'Now he can't take it,' I thought. But then I remembered something.

'Stop the cart, please,' I said, with difficulty. 'I haven't written my address on the box. I want to write it now. Stop, please.'

The cart stopped in an empty street. 'What's this?' the young man said. 'There's no name on the box. It isn't your box.'

'Yes, it is!' I shouted. The money fell out of my mouth and onto the ground.

'You've stolen that money, too,' the young man cried. He picked up my money and he jumped into the cart. 'It's mine now!' he cried and he drove away very quickly. I ran after the cart, but I could not catch him.

I had no money for the coach. So I found the road to Dover and I started walking along it.

'I need money for food,' I thought. 'I'll have to sell something. I'll sell my coat.'

I went into a shop. 'Do you want to buy a coat?' I asked.

'How much?' the man asked.

'One shilling and sixpence,' I answered.

'That's too much,' he said. 'I'll give you ninepence.' I gave him the coat and took the ninepence. I bought food with it and walked on. Then night came and I slept in a field.

The next day was Sunday and I reached a town not far from London. I was pleased that the streets were almost empty. I was very dirty and I did not want to see people. I slept outside again.

In the morning I was very hungry, so I sold my shoes. I did not get much money for them. I was now wearing only my shirt and trousers. I was tired, cold and very dirty.

At last I reached Dover. 'Do you know Miss Trotwood?' I asked a man.

'No,' he said. 'Go away!'

I went into a shop. 'Go away, you dirty boy!' the shopkeeper shouted.

'Please!' I cried. 'Do you know Miss Trotwood?'

'Yes,' one of the customers said. 'You're lucky. I'm her servant.' She took me to my aunt's house.

'Wait outside,' she said.

My aunt came out. 'What do you want?' she asked. 'Go away! I don't like dirty little boys. No boys here!'

'Please, Aunt,' I said. 'I'm David Copperfield! You came to my mother's house on the night I was born. Now she's dead and I'm very unhappy. I went to work, but I ran away. I've walked from London, sleeping outside.' I was crying now.

'What?' my aunt shouted. She sat on the ground for a moment and then jumped up again. 'This is a surprise!' she cried. 'Come in! Come into the house!' When we were in the house, my aunt looked at me. 'You're very dirty,' she said. 'You need a bath.'

I had a bath and we ate dinner together. Janet, the servant, burned my clothes and found me new ones. My aunt and I talked about Mr Murdstone.

'Do I have to go back to him?' I asked.

'I don't know,' my aunt said, quite kindly. 'I'll tell you tomorrow. Go to bed now.'

So I went to bed and slept very well.

Chapter 6   I Make a New Start

Next morning my aunt sat with me while I was eating breakfast. She looked at me without speaking. Then she said, 'I have written to Mr Murdstone.'

'Oh?' I said. I felt rather afraid.

'He'll come here soon,' she said.

'Will he take me away?' I asked.

'I don't know,' she said. 'Have you finished your breakfast?'

'Yes,' I answered.

'It's a nice day,' she said. 'Go outside and play.'

Some days later we were sitting together, looking out of the window. The garden looked beautiful in the sun. Suddenly my aunt stood up. 'Janet!' she shouted. 'There's a donkey in the garden! It's damaging the grass!' She ran out of the room.

The rider of the donkey was Miss Murdstone, but my aunt did

not know her. She ran to the animal and pulled it back towards the road. 'Get off my grass!' she shouted at Miss Murdstone. 'What do you think you are doing in my garden? This is my grass. Don't ride on it.'

I ran outside, too. 'It's Miss Murdstone, Aunt!' I shouted. My aunt did not listen. 'Get off the grass!' she cried again.

'It's Miss Murdstone!' I repeated at the top of my voice. 'And Mr Murdstone!'

'Oh!' my aunt said. She looked angry. 'Come into the house,' she said. She walked quickly inside and we all followed her.

Mr Murdstone and his sister sat down. My aunt looked at them.

'So you married little Clara,' she said. 'The poor child!' Mr Murdstone looked very angry. He looked at me.

'David is a bad boy,' he said. 'He has no money of his own, so I found him a job. He never thanked me for this. What did he do? He ran away. But now he has to go back there and earn his living.'

'Oh, no, Aunt!' I cried. 'I hate that place.'

'If he doesn't return to London today,' Mr Murdstone continued, 'I won't see him again. I won't help him. I won't speak to him again. And I won't give him any money.'

'You haven't helped him!' my aunt said angrily. 'He can stay here with me. Please go now.'

'I'll be happy to go,' said Mr Murdstone. 'But you're making a big mistake. He's a terrible child.'

'And you are a terrible man, Mr Murdstone,' my aunt said coldly. 'You were unkind to David's mother and you made her very unhappy. You and your sister are cruel and unfeeling people.'

'*You're* a very rude woman!' Miss Murdstone shouted.

'You!' my aunt said. 'Be quiet! Get out of my house! Go away and don't ride donkeys on my grass again!' The Murdstones left the house angrily.

'Get off my grass!'

'This is your home now, David,' my aunt said. 'You can stay here for as long as you like.'

'Thank you, Aunt,' I said. 'Oh, thank you!' I kissed her.

'Let me think,' she said. 'Now you needn't work, but you should go to school again. I know – you can go to school in Canterbury. We'll visit Mr Wickfield there.'

'Mr Wickfield?' I said. 'Who is he?'

'He's a lawyer,' she said. 'He's a clever lawyer and my friend, too. He manages my money. He can suggest a good school.'

We went to Canterbury in my aunt's carriage and stopped outside Mr Wickfield's office. A face looked out at us through the window. It was a thin, white face with red eyes. My aunt told me that the face belonged to Uriah Heep, Mr Wickfield's clerk. He came out of the office and held the horse's head. We went into the office, where we met Mr Wickfield. He was a large man with a red face and white hair.

'Good morning, Miss Trotwood,' he said politely. 'What can I do for you?'

'I want a school for David,' my aunt said. 'He's poor David Copperfield's son and I'm looking after him now. I want him to become happy and useful. Do you know a good school?'

'Yes, I do,' he said. 'David can go there tomorrow if you like.'

'Tomorrow?' she said. She never took long to decide anything. 'That's fine. Where can he stay today?'

'He can stay here,' Mr Wickfield said. It was a beautiful house and I was quite happy about this.

My aunt left and I stayed in Canterbury. In the afternoon I went back into Mr Wickfield's office. Uriah Heep was there. He looked at me from time to time but he did not speak. He was very thin and he wore black clothes. When he was not working, he rubbed his large, thin hands together. I did not like him. When he went home, he said, 'Good night, Mr Copperfield,' and shook my hand. His own hand was cold and wet. It felt like touching a dead fish.

I ate dinner with Mr Wickfield and his daughter. She was very pretty and calm. I liked her.

'This is Agnes,' Mr Wickfield said. He held her hand and smiled at her. He clearly loved her very much.

In the morning I went to the school, where I was put in the lowest class. I stayed there all day but I was too uncomfortable to make friends. I returned to Mr Wickfield's house at night and we all had dinner together. Then Agnes went to her room and Mr Wickfield talked to me.

'Where will you stay, David?' he asked.

'Can I stay here?' I said.

'Yes, you can,' he said. 'But it's rather dull here. Young people don't usually like dull places.'

'But I like this house,' I said. 'Agnes lives here and she is young.'

'Agnes?' he said. 'Is it dull for her? I never thought about that before. Her mother is dead, you see and—' He started to drink his wine and he did not speak again.

Uriah Heep was in the office reading, even at this late hour. I went in to see him.

'What are you reading?' I asked.

'I'm studying law,' he said. 'This is a law book.'

'Do you want to be a lawyer?' I asked.

'Yes,' he said. 'Lawyers earn a lot of money, don't they?'

'I don't know,' I said. 'But I'm sure that you're very clever.'

'Oh, no,' he said. 'I'm very humble. My family is humble, too. My father's dead but he was a very humble man. My mother is humble. But I can be a lawyer; Mr Wickfield is helping me. He's a good man and I am very lucky.' Uriah rubbed his hands together in that ugly way of his. He was an ugly man. 'Miss Agnes is good to me, too,' he continued. 'I like Miss Agnes. She's very pretty, isn't she?' He looked at his watch and rubbed his hands again. 'I have to go home now,' he said. 'Come and see my humble house one day. Come and meet my mother.'

'Thank you,' I said. 'I will.'

He went home and I went to bed. I dreamed about Uriah, who frightened me.

The new school was very different from the old one. I began to like it very much and soon had many friends.

Chapter 7   I Finish My Education

I was walking back to Mr Wickfield's house one day when I met Uriah. 'This *is* a nice surprise, Mr Copperfield,' he said. 'I'm going home now. Why don't you come with me and meet my mother?'

I did not want to go but I walked with him. 'How are your law studies?' I asked.

'I'm learning a lot,' he said. 'But it's very difficult. Some of the words in the books are in Latin and I don't know Latin.'

'I know Latin,' I said. 'I'll teach you.'

'Oh, no, Mr Copperfield.' Uriah rubbed his hands together. 'I'm very humble. Humble people can't learn Latin. That's only for gentlemen.'

Mrs Heep looked like her son. She was thin and her clothes were black, too. I sat in their house and they asked me a lot of questions. They asked me about my family and about London. I did not tell them about my job in London. They talked about Mr Wickfield and Agnes.

'Mr Wickfield drinks a lot of wine,' Mrs Heep said. 'That's very bad for him, isn't it?'

'I don't know,' I said. I did not like Mrs Heep very much.

A man was passing the open door of the Heeps' house and he stopped outside.

'Copperfield! My boy!' he cried. 'I thought it was you!'

It was Mr Micawber and he came in. I introduced him to Uriah and Mrs Heep and he shook their hands. I felt very uncomfortable. I did not want Mr Micawber to talk about London, where I was poor and unimportant. The Heeps thought that I was a gentleman.

But he did not talk about London. He talked about Mrs Micawber and his family. Then, when he was leaving, he invited me to dinner at his hotel the next day.

Before our meeting I saw Mr Micawber in the street with Uriah. They were having friendly conversation together.

At dinner that night I asked Mr Micawber about Uriah.

'He's a clever man,' Mr Micawber said. 'I like him. I need someone like him to manage my money.'

Mrs Micawber was eating with us and she told me about Plymouth. 'My family did not like Mr Micawber,' she said. 'He owed too much money. So we came to Canterbury. Mr Micawber will find work here. We are waiting for some money that other people owe us. But it will come soon.'

After dinner, we drank a lot of wine. Mr Micawber became very happy and we sang songs together.

But the next day I received a letter. It said, 'My dear young friend. The money has not come. I owe a lot of money in Canterbury so I am leaving today. I try hard, but I always seem to fail. We shall not meet again. Wilkins Micawber.'

◆

I worked hard at school and the years passed quickly. Agnes was always kind and calm and I liked her very much. She became like a sister to me. Mr Wickfield drank too much and spent too little time working. Uriah worked hard in the office and knew a lot about Mr Wickfield's work.

At last I finished school. 'What will you do now?' my aunt asked.

'I don't know,' I said. 'I should find a job. What kind of work can I do?'

'Have a holiday first,' she suggested. 'Then you can think about work. Visit Peggotty.'

'I will,' I agreed. 'I'll go to Yarmouth.'

But I travelled to London first by coach. I wore new clothes and I looked fine. I felt like a gentleman and I was very happy.

On the first day I went to a hotel and ordered dinner. I noticed a young man eating dinner at another table. I looked at him for a moment in surprise. Then I went to say hello.

'Do you remember me?' I asked. He stood up.

'No,' he said. 'No, I don't think—' Then he shouted, 'Copperfield!' It was Steerforth.

We ate breakfast together next morning. 'You haven't changed,' Steerforth said. 'You're a man now, but you look very young. Come with me. Come and stay at my house.'

'But I'm going to Yarmouth,' I said.

'Don't go,' he said. 'Stay with me tonight and go to Yarmouth tomorrow.'

I laughed. 'I can't say "No" to you, Steerforth,' I told him. 'I'll be happy to stay with you.'

Steerforth lived with his mother in Highgate, to the north of London. His mother was tall, quite old and very proud. A strange woman called Rosa Dartle lived with her. I felt uncomfortable with her from the time of our first meeting. She had cruel eyes and a scar on her face. The scar was an ugly white mark near her mouth.

We talked about the people in Yarmouth.

'Are they like us?' Mrs Steerforth asked.

'No,' Steerforth said. 'They are rather rough and rude.'

I did not think that this was true. My friends there were not rough. But I did not say anything. Later I asked Steerforth about Rosa Dartle.

'Where did she get that scar?' I asked. Steerforth looked angry and sad. 'I gave her that,' he said.

'When?'

'I was only a little boy,' he said. 'I threw something at her. It hit her on the mouth. I was very sorry.'

I stayed there for a few days. When I went to Yarmouth, Steerforth travelled with me.

I left Steerforth at the hotel and hurried across the town to see Peggotty.

When I got to Barkis's house, Peggotty was there. She did not know me, though, and she looked at me in surprise.

'Peggotty!' I said. 'Have I grown very big? Don't you know me?'

'David!' she shouted. 'Oh, my little David!' She put her arms round me and cried. Then she dried her eyes and we went to see Barkis. He was ill in bed but very pleased to see me. He gave Peggotty some money to prepare a special dinner. Then Steerforth arrived. He laughed a lot and we had fun together.

After an hour we left Barkis's house and we went to Mr Peggotty's. We heard Mr Peggotty shouting and laughing. When we went inside, Ham was holding Emily's hand. His face was very red and Emily was looking at the floor.

'Come in!' Mr Peggotty cried. 'I have a surprise for you. Ham and Emily are going to get married!'

'That's good,' Steerforth said. There was a strange look on his face. 'When did you hear that?'

'A minute ago,' Mr Peggotty said.

Ham began to talk. 'I loved Emily when she was a child,' he said. 'And now I love her as a woman. I know that she is younger than I am. But she has agreed to marry me and I'm a very happy man.'

We all drank wine happily together. The men talked a lot but

'Ham and Emily are going to get married!'

Emily was very quiet. She often looked at Steerforth. Time passed quickly and soon it was late. 'It's time to go,' Steerforth said. We shook hands with them all and said goodbye. Steerforth and I walked back to the hotel.

'I'm sorry that they're going to be married,' Steerforth said. 'Emily is pretty and full of life. She should be a gentleman's wife. But Ham is rough and rather dull. He's just a fisherman. It's very sad.'

'You're wrong!' I cried. I did not agree with him at all. 'Ham's a good man. He'll be a good husband to Emily.'

Steerforth put his hand on my arm and smiled strangely. 'David,' he said. 'You're a good man, too. But you don't understand *me*.'

After that I stayed at Barkis's house and Steerforth stayed at the hotel. He went out with the fishermen and I did not see him often. One night I was alone in the house. I was sitting by the fire when he came in. His face was sad.

'What's wrong?' I asked.

'I was thinking,' he said.

'What?'

'My father's dead,' he said, 'and I need him now. I need a father to guide me. My mother is no use; everything I do is fine with her. I'm not a good man and that makes me unhappy.'

'I don't understand,' I said. 'What are you talking about?'

'Oh, it isn't important,' he said. 'See, I'm happier, now. Let's go for a walk.' He stood up and smiled.

'I've bought a boat,' he told me proudly, while we were walking.

'In Yarmouth?' I asked. It was a surprise. 'But you don't often come to Yarmouth.'

'Ham's keeping the boat for me,' he said.

'There!' I said. 'You *are* good. You've given the boat to Ham.'

'I haven't *given* him the boat,' Steerforth said. 'He's looking

35

after it for me. I've called the boat *The Little Emily*.'

He looked more cheerful when I saw him after that. The time in Yarmouth was a very happy one for me but it passed quickly. Our last night came and I was walking back to Barkis's house. Ham stopped me outside.

'Please don't go in,' he said. 'Emily is talking to a woman inside. The woman has asked for help.'

A few minutes later Peggotty opened the door. 'You can come in, now,' she said. The woman was sitting next to Emily. Her name was Martha Endells and she was crying.

'I've done something terrible,' she said. 'My mother and father don't want me. The people in Yarmouth hate me. I'm going to leave and go to London. London will be better than Yarmouth.'

'What will you do in London?' Emily asked. She had her arms around the woman.

'I'll find work,' Martha told her. 'But I need money. I have nothing.'

'Here's money,' Emily said. 'You can go to London.'

'Thank you,' Martha said. 'You're very kind. I'll always remember you.'

She left the house. Emily closed the door behind her. Her face was sad and she began to cry, too. 'I'm like Martha,' she said. 'I'm bad, too.'

'You?' Ham said. 'You're not bad. You're beautiful and good.'

'No, I'm not,' Emily said. 'I'm so unhappy. Please help me, Ham. I want to be good.'

Ham put his arms round her and soon she was quiet. She was talking like Steerforth. I did not understand Emily and Steerforth then. But I understood later.

Chapter 8   I Meet the Girl of My Dreams

When we returned to London, my aunt was waiting for me. I told her that I wanted to be a lawyer. So she paid one thousand pounds to Spenlow and Jorkins; Mr Spenlow was going to teach me law. My aunt also found me rooms in the home of a Mrs Crupp, who cleaned the rooms and cooked for me.

London is a lonely place and I felt very alone. Steerforth did not visit me and I hadn't any friends. But one day I met him in the street with two of his friends. I gave them my address and asked them to come to dinner.

It was a good dinner but I drank too much. I became very silly.

'The theatre's a fine place!' I cried. 'Let's go there.'

We went to the theatre. Outside the main entrance, Steerforth's friends held my arms; I could not stand by myself. Then they helped me into the building.

'Let's sit here,' Steerforth suggested. I fell into my seat, laughing.

'Oh!' a voice said. A girl was sitting next to me and I looked at her. But I was drunk and I could not see her well.

'David!' the girl said.

'Agnes!' I replied. I could not speak clearly. 'What a surprise!'

'Oh, David,' Agnes said. 'Look at you. Please go home. Please go home and go to bed.'

'Yes,' I said, feeling like a small boy. 'Yes, I will.'

I left the theatre noisily. Steerforth had to carry me to my rooms and put me to bed.

The next morning I felt very ill. I remembered Agnes and I felt even worse. But she sent me a letter. I read it nervously. It said, 'My dear David, I am staying at the house of a man who works with my father, Mr Waterbrook, in Ely Place, Holborn. Will you come and see me today? I shall be in all day. With love, Agnes.'

I did not want to see Agnes after the night before, but I went to the house. Agnes was not angry with me. When she saw me, she smiled.

'Good morning, David,' she said.

'Oh, Agnes,' I said, 'I'm very sorry that I was drunk at the theatre. I was very stupid. Please forgive me.'

'I have forgiven you,' Agnes said. 'Don't think about the theatre. Don't be sorry about that. But you have a bad friend.'

'A bad friend?' I said. 'Who is he?'

'Steerforth,' Agnes said. 'He isn't a good man.'

'Oh, Agnes,' I said, 'he *is*! Steerforth is my best friend!'

'I'm sorry,' Agnes said. 'I don't like him.' She smiled. 'Now, I want you to forgive *me*,' she said. 'I've been rude.'

'No, you haven't,' I said. 'But we won't talk about Steerforth.'

'No, we won't,' Agnes said. 'David, have you seen Uriah?'

'No,' I said. 'Uriah Heep? Is he in London?'

'Yes,' she said. Her face was unhappy. 'Uriah owns half my father's business now. Did you know that?'

'No!' I shouted. 'Uriah? It can't be true!'

'It is,' Agnes said. 'Because my father always drank a lot, he couldn't manage the business. Uriah helped him. After a time, my father was not able to do anything without Uriah's help, so he gave him half the business.' Agnes began to cry.

'Uriah Heep!' I said. 'The dog! I hate the man! But please don't cry, Agnes.'

Agnes dried her eyes. Then Mrs Waterbrook came into the room. She shook hands with me. 'Will you stay to dinner, Mr Copperfield?' she asked.

'Yes, please,' I replied.

A lot of people came to dinner but it was a very dull meal. Nobody talked to me and I did not sit near Agnes. Uriah Heep was also sitting at the other end of the table. Then I heard the name "Traddles".

It was my old friend. I introduced myself to him again and we talked about Salem House. He met Agnes and I told her about him. I was very happy to see him again.

After dinner Uriah Heep came up to me and suggested a walk. I was too afraid of him to refuse. We walked away from the house and I asked him about the business and Mr Wickfield.

'He was ill,' Uriah said. 'He drinks a lot, you know. He lost money and he needed help. I wanted to help Miss Agnes, too. She's pretty, isn't she? When will she marry? Who will she marry?' There was an ugly smile on his face. I knew then that he wanted to marry her. I was very angry with him but I did not say anything. He could hurt Mr Wickfield and Agnes now.

◆

There were very few dinner parties and I was often lonely. Steerforth was at university in Oxford and I did not see Traddles again. Every day I went to Mr Spenlow's office and he taught me about the law.

One day he invited me to his house. He lived just outside London. I thanked him and accepted.

'Stay the night,' he suggested. 'Stay for Saturday and Sunday.'

'That will be nice,' I agreed.

'We'll go together in my carriage,' he said.

We went to Mr Spenlow's house on the Saturday. It was a big house with a large garden. We went inside. There were two women there but I only saw one of them. After my eyes fell on her, I could not look away. She was beautiful.

'This is my daughter, Dora, Mr Copperfield,' Mr Spenlow said. 'And this is Miss Murdstone. She is company for my daughter and looks after her.'

'I have met Miss Murdstone before,' I said. 'How are you, Miss Murdstone?'

'Very well, thank you,' Miss Murdstone said coldly.

I went to my room and thought about Dora. Her hair was beautiful and her face was like the sun in a dark sky. When I went down to dinner, I could not eat. People talked to me but I did not hear them. My eyes stayed on Dora.

After dinner Miss Murdstone spoke to me. 'Mr Copperfield,' she said.

'Yes, Miss Murdstone?'

'You know that I don't like you,' she said. 'And I don't like your aunt. I know that you don't like me.'

'That is true,' I said.

'But we will be polite in this house,' she said.

'Yes, we will,' I agreed. 'Good night.'

I went to bed and I dreamed about Dora. I had beautiful dreams. Next morning I got up early and walked in the garden. Dora was out there too.

'Good morning,' she said. She had a pretty voice.

'Good morning,' I said. 'You've just been to France, haven't you, Miss Dora?'

'Yes,' she answered. 'Have you been there?'

'No,' I said with feeling. 'I want to stay here. I want to stay in England.'

'Stay in England?' she said. 'Why?'

'*You* are here,' I said. '*You* are in England.'

'Oh, Mr Copperfield!' Her face was red but she laughed. She spoke to the little dog that she was holding. 'Mr Copperfield says nice things, doesn't he, Jip?' she said softly.

'Come, Mr Copperfield, let's look at the flowers.' She guided me through the garden. Dora looked at the flowers and I looked at Dora. She was prettier than the flowers.

'Is Miss Murdstone a friend of yours?' she asked.

'No,' I said.

'Good,' Dora said. 'I don't like her. She follows me and watches me all the time.' She kissed her little dog. 'Doesn't she, Jip?'

She was prettier than the flowers.

We talked together and then Miss Murdstone joined us. 'Good morning,' she said. 'Come into the house now and we will have breakfast.'

I will always remember that Sunday as a very happy day for me. I sat with Dora and talked to her. Miss Murdstone was there in the room but I soon forgot about her. She could not make me unhappy.

After my return to London, I spent hours each day walking up and down the streets. I was hoping to see Dora. Once I did see her in her carriage. She smiled at me and I felt better.

Mrs Crupp saw the change in me. My thoughts were always far away.

'Aren't you well, Mr Copperfield?' she asked kindly.

'Yes, I'm well,' I told her.

'I know,' Mrs Crupp said. 'I know about young men. You've met a pretty girl, Mr Copperfield. You're in love.'

Chapter 9   I See Old Friends

I felt lonely, so I decided to visit Traddles. He lived in a poor house in a poor street. I walked up the stairs and pulled the bell. Traddles opened the door.

'Copperfield! My dear man!' he cried. 'Come in. This is nice. I don't often have visitors. In fact you are my only visitor this month.'

His room was not very big. There was a small table in one corner with pens and paper on it.

'What are you doing?' I asked.

'I'm studying law,' he said. 'When I left school, I didn't have any money. So I worked hard and earned some. I paid that to a lawyer, who is teaching me.'

'When will you finish?' I asked. 'When will you be a lawyer?'

'I don't know,' Traddles said. 'It will be a long time.' He looked rather unhappy. 'I want to marry, but Sophy and I will have to wait.' Then he looked more cheerful and he laughed. 'But she's a good girl. She's pretty and kind, too. We can wait. I love her very much and she loves me.'

'I'm pleased for you,' I said, and I really meant it.

'I don't like this room,' he continued. 'But it doesn't cost much and I have a nice neighbour.'

'Hello!' a voice called outside.

'Who's that?' I asked.

'That's my neighbour,' Traddles said. 'His name's Micawber.' Mr Micawber came into the room. 'Copperfield, my boy!' he cried. 'This is a surprise!' He took my hands and looked at me. 'Mrs Micawber will be pleased.'

'How are you, Mr Micawber?' I asked.

'We are rather poor,' he said. 'But we have a good friend here – Mr Traddles. And we are hoping for money soon. We are always hoping.' He laughed happily.

I was happy to see Mr Micawber again and I invited the Micawbers and Traddles to my house. They came for dinner. Mr Micawber made us a drink from wine and fruit. He sang loudly while he was making it. The drink tasted good. Then the dinner arrived, and it was terrible. 'Mrs Crupp hasn't cooked this meat well,' I said. 'It's red in the middle. I'm very sorry.'

'Don't worry, Copperfield,' Mr Micawber said. 'We'll cut the meat into pieces and cook it again on the fire.'

He did it himself, and it tasted very good. We drank more wine and sang songs. We had a very happy time together.

'What are you doing now?' I asked Mr Micawber.

'I haven't got a job,' he said sadly. 'But I'll get one soon.'

'Can't you borrow some money?' I asked.

'I have borrowed some,' he said. 'But I've spent it.' He smiled. 'You've grown into a fine young man, Copperfield,' he said, changing the subject. 'Will you marry? Do you know a nice girl?'

'Yes, I do,' I said.

'Good,' he said. 'Is she pretty?'

'She's very beautiful,' I told him.

It grew late and they left. When Mrs Micawber and Traddles went out, Mr Micawber stayed behind. He gave me a letter. 'Don't read it now,' he said. 'You can read it when I've gone.'

I went into my room but then I heard a noise on the stairs. 'David!' a voice called. 'Are you there?' It was Steerforth. He came straight in. 'I've surprised you,' he said cheerfully, and he laughed. He looked at the table. 'Ah!' he said, 'you've had a dinner with friends. You always have a lot of fun.'

'Yes,' I said. 'They were old friends. Do you remember Traddles?'

'Traddles?' he said. 'No, I don't remember him.'

'He was at school with us,' I said.

'Oh yes,' Steerforth said. 'Traddles. He was a stupid boy.'

'Where have you been?' I asked. I did not agree with his opinion of Traddles.

'I've been in Yarmouth,' he said. 'Emily is going to marry Ham soon. Oh! I have a letter for you. It's from Peggotty. Barkis is very ill. In fact, he's dying.'

I read the letter. 'Peggotty is very unhappy,' I said slowly. 'I'll have to go to Yarmouth. She wants to see me.'

'Come to Highgate first,' Steerforth said. 'Come and see my mother and Rosa. They want to see you.'

'But I need to go to Yarmouth,' I said.

'Well, don't go tomorrow,' Steerforth said. 'Come to Highgate first.'

'All right, I will,' I agreed.

'I'll go home now,' Steerforth said. 'Walk with me some of the way.' I went out with Steerforth. In the streets we walked and talked. He seemed excited and perhaps a little drunk. Then I left him and returned home. There I read Mr Micawber's letter.

'Dear Copperfield,' the letter said, 'I have lost all my money. I borrowed money from Traddles and I have lost his money too. Now I have nothing. I have hurt Traddles and I am very sorry about that. He is a good friend. I will not see you again. Wilkins Micawber.' I felt very sad about Traddles and I felt sorry for Mr Micawber, too. But there was nothing I could do.

I asked Mr Spenlow for a holiday and I went to Highgate.

Rosa Dartle was there when I arrived. 'I know Steerforth well,' she said, looking worried. 'He is acting very strangely at the moment. What is he doing? What has he done in Yarmouth?'

'I don't know,' I said. I could not imagine what the problem was.

'It's very strange,' she said. 'I don't like it.'

That night we all had dinner together. 'Why are you unhappy, Rosa?' Steerforth asked. 'Don't be unhappy. You have a pretty voice; sing to us.'

Rosa sang. When she finished, Steerforth went to her. 'That was beautiful,' he said and touched her hair.

'Don't touch me!' she cried. 'Don't touch me!' She ran out of the room.

'What's wrong with her?' I asked Steerforth.

'I don't know,' he said. He did not seem very worried.

'I'm going early tomorrow,' I told him. 'So I'll say good night now.'

'Good night, David,' said Steerforth and he smiled at me. It was a sad smile. 'Don't forget me. I'm not really a bad man – remember that.'

'I will,' I said. 'I'll always remember you. You're my best friend.'

'Don't touch me!' she cried. 'Don't touch me!'

Chapter 10   I Find a Wife

I went to Yarmouth but I was too late. When I reached Yarmouth, Barkis was already dead. I spent some time with Peggotty talking about poor Barkis. He had a lot of money which was hidden under his bed. He left a thousand pounds to Mr Peggotty and two thousand to his wife – Peggotty, my dear friend.

Then I left her and went to visit her brother. The night was cold and wet, but Mr Peggotty's house was warm and comfortable. A big fire was burning and there was a light in the window. Mrs Gummidge was complaining to Mr Peggotty that she was lonely.

'Don't be unhappy,' Mr Peggotty told her. 'Emily will come soon. She'll make you feel better.'

The door opened and Ham came in. He was wearing a big hat and we could not see his face. 'Mr David,' he said in a strange voice. 'Come outside, please.'

I followed him out of the house. 'What's wrong?' I asked.

'It's Emily,' he said. He looked very pale.

'Emily?' I cried. 'Is she ill?'

'No, she's not ill,' Ham said slowly. 'She's gone.'

'Gone? Where?' I cried.

'She's gone away,' Ham said. He turned his face away from me. 'What can I say to Mr Peggotty?' he asked. 'How can I tell him?'

Mr Peggotty came out of the house at that moment. He saw Ham's white face and mine. 'Ham!' he shouted. 'Emily! Where is Emily?' He fell back against the wall and we both helped him inside.

'Here's a letter, Mr David,' Ham said, pulling it from his coat pocket. 'Read it, I can't read it again.'

The letter was very short. It said, 'When you read this, I shall be far away. I will only return if he makes me a lady. Please believe that I am suffering. I can't marry you. Remember me and

47

forgive me. I love you all with all my heart. I am very sorry. Emily.'

Mr Peggotty sat down hard in a chair. His face was red and he was very angry. 'Who's the man?' he cried. 'Who is he? Tell me! I want to know!'

'It's Steerforth,' Ham said quietly. 'She's gone with Steerforth.'

'Steerforth!' I cried. 'And I brought him to this house. When did they go?' I asked Ham.

'This evening,' he said. 'They left this evening in Steerforth's carriage.'

'Give me my coat,' Mr Peggotty said, standing up again with difficulty.

'Where are you going?' Mrs Gummidge asked.

'I'm going to find Emily,' Mr Peggotty said. 'I'll break Steerforth's boat into little pieces and then I'll travel to the ends of the earth. I have to find her!'

'No, Daniel,' Mrs Gummidge said. 'Don't go now. You're excited and you'll only get ill. Listen to me. I'm not the most cheerful person, I know that. I'm never much help to you. But I'll stop complaining now and help you. Stay here tonight.' She took Mr Peggotty's arm and he sat down again. Then he put his head in his hands and he began to cry. I could not help, so I went back to my hotel. One name stuck in my head. Steerforth!

After that night Mrs Gummidge changed. She became a completely different person. She cleaned the house and prepared Mr Peggotty's clothes for his journey.

'I shall leave tomorrow,' he told me. 'I'll go to London and start there. I *will* find Emily again!'

Next morning he and I went to the coach. Ham and Mrs Gummidge came with us to say goodbye. Peggotty joined us, because she planned to travel to London too. Ham stopped me while I was climbing into the coach.

'Mr David,' he said. 'If Mr Peggotty needs money, he should

ask me. Please tell him that.'

'I will,' I said. 'Mr Peggotty is not poor now – he has money from Barkis. But I'll tell him.'

The coach began to move, and Mrs Gummidge ran behind it. 'Goodbye, Daniel!' she shouted to Mr Peggotty. 'Don't be sad, and don't worry. You will find Emily. I'll look after the house. When you come back, I'll be here. Goodbye!'

We reached London and found a room for Mr Peggotty and his sister. I wanted to see Mrs Steerforth, so I went to Highgate. She knew about Steerforth and Emily. I told her about Mr Peggotty's unhappiness.

'What does he want?' she asked. 'I don't want to see him.' She looked proud and angry. Then she changed her mind. 'No. Wait. I'll see him. Bring him here tomorrow.'

The next day we visited her together. Mrs Steerforth sat very straight in her chair and Rosa Dartle stayed with her.

'You are the girl's uncle, aren't you?' said Mrs Steerforth proudly.

'I am.' Mr Peggotty spoke quietly. He was polite and he was not afraid of her.

'My son won't marry Emily,' Mrs Steerforth told him. 'She isn't a lady.'

'She's a clever girl,' Mr Peggotty said. 'She'll become a lady if he marries her.'

'He will *not* marry her,' she told him. 'I know my son.'

'When he came to our house, we were always kind to him,' Mr Peggotty said. 'We thought that he was our friend. Now he has done this cruel thing. He has deceived us.'

'My son does not deceive people,' Mrs Steerforth said proudly. 'He is a gentleman. But you are unhappy and you don't understand him. I feel sorry for you, so I'll give you some money for your trouble.'

'No!' Mr Peggotty cried. 'I don't want your money. And I am

49

sorry for *you*, Mrs Steerforth. Your son has deceived you, too. I'll leave you now. You can't help me.'

I followed him out of the room but Rosa stopped me on the stairs.

'It was you!' she cried angrily. 'You took him to that house. *You* took him to those rough, rude people.'

'Emily isn't rude and she isn't rough!' I said. 'And Mr Peggotty is a good, kind man. Steerforth has hurt them terribly.'

'I hate her!' Rosa cried. 'I hate that girl!'

When I was leaving the house, I looked back. Rosa stood at the door. Her face was white and angry and I could see her scar clearly. It looked very ugly.

So Mr Peggotty started on his journey. He went away to look for Emily. I felt very sorry for him, but I was not always sad. I saw Mr Spenlow every day. Each time I saw him, I thought about Dora again.

One day he said, 'You remember my daughter, Mr Copperfield, don't you?'

Remember her? How could I forget her? But I only replied, 'Miss Dora? Yes. Why, sir?'

'She wants to have a party,' he said. 'Do you like parties? Can you come?'

Could I go? Mr Spenlow did not need to ask. But he did not know this and I did not tell him.

'Yes, Mr Spenlow,' I said. 'You're very kind. When is the party?'

'It's next week,' he said, and he told me the date. 'You won't forget, will you?'

'No,' I promised. 'No, I won't forget.'

Dora wrote to me, too. 'Please come,' the letter said. I carried it near to my heart. The week passed very slowly, but the day came in the end. I bought new clothes and some flowers for Dora. Then I went to her house.

She was sitting in the garden with a friend, Julia Mills. Jip, the little dog, was there too. I was very pleased that Miss Murdstone was not outside. Dora liked the flowers I gave her. She showed them to Jip.

'Smell these flowers, Jip!' she said. 'Aren't they pretty?'

Jip bit them and broke some in half.

'Don't do that, Jip!' Dora cried. 'Don't hurt the beautiful flowers! Mr Copperfield brought them!'

At least Dora liked my flowers. 'Perhaps she likes me, too,' I thought happily. But I did not say this to her.

We drove into the country for the party. Dora, Julia and Mr Spenlow drove in a carriage and I rode on a horse. A lot of other people joined us; most of them were Dora's friends and neighbours. We stopped near some trees with a view over hills and fields. The fields were full of flowers, and it was a beautiful day. We got out the food and the wine.

I was sorry that I could not sit near Dora. A young man sat next to her and made her laugh. But I was next to a very pretty girl. I saw that Dora was watching us. She stopped laughing, and I felt better.

After the meal Julia brought Dora to me.

'Dora is unhappy,' Julia said.

'Why?' I asked.

'You talked to Miss Kitt but you didn't talk to me,' Dora complained.

'But I couldn't talk to you,' I said. 'You were busy talking to another man.'

'I'm sorry,' Dora said. 'Talk to me now. Stay by my side.'

So I stayed with Dora. She sang songs and talked to me. Then she went home in her carriage. I rode next to the carriage on my horse. Mr Spenlow was asleep, so I was able to continue my conversation with Dora. I was very happy on that journey.

We reached her house and I felt sad again.

'I should go home,' I said. 'When will we meet again?'

I rode next to the carriage on my horse.

'I don't know,' Dora said. 'Soon, I hope.'

'Listen!' Miss Mills said. 'Next week Dora is coming to my house. You can visit her there. I won't invite Miss Murdstone.'

'Thank you, Miss Julia!' I said. 'You are a good friend.'

A week later I went to Miss Julia's house. A servant opened the door.

'Is Mr Mills at home?' I said.

'No,' the servant said, 'but Miss Mills is here. Come in, please.'

I followed the servant upstairs. Dora and Julia were sitting there together, but Julia soon left us.

Dora looked at me and smiled. I walked straight across the room and took her in my arms.

'Dora!' I said. 'I love you! Will you marry me?'

'Oh, David!' she said. 'I love you, too. Yes, I will marry you.'

She started crying with happiness and I held her tighter. It was the best moment of my life.

When Dora stopped crying, we sat quietly together for a time. Then Dora spoke.

'We won't tell my father yet,' she said.

'Why?' I asked. I wanted to tell the world.

'He will be angry,' she said. 'You need to find the right time and ask his permission.'

'All right, we won't tell him yet,' I agreed. Then Julia came back and we told her the good news. She was very pleased.

After that day I did not see Dora often. But I wrote letters to her and she wrote letters to me. I was very happy.

Chapter 11   I Am Given Bad News

A few things were worrying me, though. One night I received another letter from Mr Micawber. This was an invitation to an area of London where he was living as "Mr Mortimer". I was not pleased by his news.

'Ah, my dear Copperfield!' he said. 'Come in! I have something to tell you. My troubles are over.'

'I'm happy for you,' I said. 'Why is that?'

'We're going to Canterbury,' Mrs Micawber said.

'Oh, yes,' I said with interest. 'What are you going to do there, Mr Micawber?'

'Mr Heep has work for me,' said Mr Micawber proudly.

'Heep?' I said. 'Uriah?'

'Yes,' he said. He smiled happily. 'It's a good job. If I do the job well, one day perhaps I'll be a lawyer too.'

I went home and thought about this news. It was a surprise and I was frightened for Mr Micawber. My fear was that Uriah was going to use and hurt him.

I had a surprise the next day, too. When I arrived home from Mr Spenlow's office, my aunt was sitting in my room.

'Hello, Aunt Betsey,' I said. 'This *is* a nice surprise. But why have you come to London? I thought that you didn't like London.'

'I don't!' she agreed. She was sitting on her box and she looked very uncomfortable.

'What's wrong, Aunt?' I asked.

'David,' my aunt said. 'I'm a very stupid old woman.'

'Why?' I asked, helping her to a chair.

'I've lost all my money,' she said. 'I've got nothing at all. Can I stay here with you?'

'Yes, of course,' I said quickly. I was very surprised and sad for her. I am afraid that I also felt very sorry for myself. 'Please do.'

We ate together and then my aunt went to bed. Later, I went to bed too, but I could not sleep. I was a poor man now. Could a poor man marry Dora? How could I ask Dora's father for his permission to marry her? But Dora was good and kind, and I was going to be a lawyer one day. Perhaps Dora was prepared to wait. I needed a job to earn the money for my studies.

Next morning I went to Mr Spenlow. 'My aunt has lost all her money,' I told him. 'She's poor now and I am too. I can't study with you. Can you please give my aunt some of her thousand pounds back?'

'Oh, dear!' Mr Spenlow cried. 'That's sad news. Let me think. *I* can give you some of the thousand pounds. But there are two of us in this business and Mr Jorkins is a very hard man. He won't give your aunt the money back. He won't let *me* give her the money!'

'Oh!' I said. 'I'm sorry.' I did not believe Mr Spenlow. I knew Mr Jorkins and he was not a hard man. But I said nothing and I left the office.

'I won't get that money,' I thought.

In the street I heard a voice calling my name. It was Agnes in her carriage.

'I was waiting for you,' she said. 'I heard the news about your aunt and I'm very sorry. David . . . ?'

'Yes?' I asked.

'My father didn't lose your aunt's money, did he?' she asked.

'I don't know,' I said. 'Let's go and see her. We can ask.'

I got into the carriage with Agnes. 'Mrs Heep and Uriah are living with us now,' she told me. 'And Father has changed. He's like Uriah's servant. It makes me angry but I can't say anything.'

We reached my rooms and went inside. 'Good morning, Agnes,' said my aunt. 'Why are you in London?'

'I'm worried about my father,' Agnes answered. 'Can I ask you a question?'

'Yes, of course,' my aunt said. 'What is it?'

'Did he lose your money?'

'Oh, no,' my aunt said. 'I lost the money. I'm a stupid old woman. Your father wanted me to save for the future but I lost it.'

'I'm pleased,' said Agnes. 'I'm pleased for him but I'm very sorry for you. And I can help you. I know a man with a job for you, David. You can earn some money.'

'Good,' I said. 'I need it. I'll work hard, I promise.'

'I know that,' Agnes said. 'You can start tomorrow.'

I left Agnes with my aunt. I went to see Dora, who was staying with Julia Mills. I waited outside until Mr Mills, Julia's father, came out. Then I went in.

'Dora,' I said. 'You look beautiful!'

'Thank you, David,' she said. 'Jip! Kiss David!' She held up the little dog. I kissed Jip and then Dora kissed me. I sat next to her.

'Dora,' I said. 'I have some news.'

'Is it good?' she asked.

'Not very good,' I said sadly.

'Then I don't want to hear it,' she said. 'Tell me some good news.' She laughed and kissed her little dog.

'I've got to tell you,' I said. 'Dora – I'm very poor!'

'Don't be silly,' Dora said. 'Poor men are thin with dirty faces. *You* aren't poor!'

'I am,' I told her. 'My aunt has lost all her money. We've got nothing now.'

'Oh, David!' Dora cried. 'Don't say that! Poor! I'm frightened!'

'Don't worry, Dora,' I said. 'We won't be very, very poor. But we won't be able to have servants. Can you cook?'

'Cook?' Dora replied. 'Oh, no, I can't cook!'

'Can you learn?' I asked. 'We'll have to save money, too. Can you manage our home yourself?'

'Manage the house? Cook? I don't want to learn these things! Oh, David, you are so cruel!' She began to cry. 'Julia!' she shouted. 'Please come here! David is being unkind to me!'

Julia came in. She put her arms round Dora and she spoke quietly to her. Soon Dora was calm again.

'I'm sorry, Dora,' I said. 'I have made you unhappy. I won't do that again. I love you.'

'I love you, too, David,' Dora said, and she dried her eyes. 'But don't talk to me about money again.'

'I won't,' I agreed.

I was worried when I left the house. 'I need to work hard!' I thought to myself. 'Then I can earn enough for the two of us. I'll see Traddles.'

Traddles told me about shorthand. 'If you learn shorthand,' he told me, 'you can earn more money.'

'I'll do that,' I said. Traddles helped me to learn shorthand.

Very early in the morning I worked at the job Agnes found for me. Then I went to Mr Spenlow's office and I worked there all day. At night I practised my shorthand with Traddles.

One day Mr Spenlow sent for me. His face was angry and Miss Murdstone was with him.

'Copperfield!' he said. 'You have deceived me! You are not a gentleman!'

'Deceived you?' I asked in surprise.

'Yes, deceived him!' Miss Murdstone agreed. She held up some papers. 'What are these?'

'Miss Murdstone!' Mr Spenlow said loudly. 'Let me speak! Copperfield, are these your letters?'

'Yes, they are,' I said.

'Read them!' he said and he gave me the letters.

'I don't need to read them,' I said. 'I love Dora and my words came from my heart.'

'Love Dora!' Miss Murdstone said. 'You love her money!'

'Miss Murdstone!' Mr Spenlow said. 'Please be quiet.' He turned to me. 'Copperfield,' he said, 'I invited you to my house

She put her arms round Dora and she spoke quietly to her.

and you were polite and friendly to me. I thought that you were a gentleman. But you were being dishonest. You wrote love letters to my daughter. I shall not let you see her again!'

'I can't promise not to see her,' I said. 'I love your daughter and your daughter loves me. It will make her unhappy if she can't see me.'

'You are young,' Mr Spenlow said. 'I will send Dora to France again. Then you will forget her.'

'I *can't* forget her,' I told him. 'I love her!'

'Don't be silly,' Mr Spenlow said. 'Your aunt has lost her money. You are a poor man. I am quite rich. At the moment Dora will get my money when I die. But I can change that. Do you understand?'

'I understand,' I said. 'If I don't promise to forget her, you will not leave your money to Dora.'

'Exactly,' Mr Spenlow said. 'Think about it, Copperfield. Talk to your aunt. Dora cannot marry a poor man. Your aunt will understand even if you don't.'

'I'll think about it,' I said. 'But please, sir, don't be angry with Dora!'

'I won't be unkind to her,' Mr Spenlow said. 'Don't worry. You can go now. And think about your promise!'

I was very unhappy. I talked to my aunt but she could not help me. I saw Julia Mills and she felt sorry for me. But she could not help me either. That night I did not sleep.

The next morning I went to the office. The clerks were talking excitedly. 'What's wrong?' I asked.

'It's Mr Spenlow,' they said.

'Is he ill?' I asked.

'No,' they said. 'He's dead!'

'Dead!' I said. 'How?'

'He was on his way home last night,' they said. 'His horse ran away and the carriage turned over. It killed him!'

It was terrible news for Dora, but I could not see her. She was staying with her aunts in Putney. Her thoughts were of her father, not of me.

Mr Spenlow was not, in fact, a rich man. He owed people money; after that was paid, there was not a lot for Dora.

It was a bad time. I often went to Putney and I walked around the streets. But I did not see Dora. I was very worried and unhappy about the future.

Chapter 12   I Receive Help and Give Little

I grew very tired from worry. I needed a holiday, so I went to Canterbury. There I told Agnes about Dora. 'What can I do, Agnes?' I asked.

'Write a letter to the aunts,' Agnes said. 'Say that you want to visit Dora.'

'Thank you,' I said. 'That's a good idea.'

'Tell me more about Dora,' Agnes said.

'She's very pretty,' I said, 'and I love her very much. But she can't manage money and she can't cook.'

Agnes laughed. 'Don't worry, David,' she said. 'Dora's young. She'll soon learn about these things.'

'Thank you, Agnes,' I said. 'You help me a lot. You're my best friend.'

Agnes looked at me strangely and she smiled. 'I will always help you,' she said. 'I want you to know that. I'll always be your friend.'

In the evening Agnes and I talked together in her room. Mrs Heep sat with us. She did not leave us alone and I was rather angry about that. But Agnes and Mr Wickfield were afraid of Uriah and Mrs Heep, so I did not discuss Mrs Heep with them. The next night I sat with Agnes again and Mrs Heep sat with us.

'Why is she watching us so closely?' I thought. I did not like Mrs Heep and so I went for a walk.

Uriah followed me. 'Where are you going, Mr David?' he asked.

'I am going for a walk,' I said. 'I can't talk to Agnes. Your mother is always in the room with us.'

'I know,' he said.

'Why is she watching us?' I asked.

Uriah closed his red eyes and rubbed his hands together. 'Oh, Mr David!' he said. 'You are a fine young man! My mother *should* watch you.'

'Why?' I asked. 'Uriah! Why?'

'Perhaps Agnes loves you,' Uriah said. 'Perhaps you want to marry her.'

'Marry Agnes?' I said. 'I *can't* marry Agnes. I love Dora. I want to marry *her*.'

'Dora? Who is Dora?' Uriah asked. I told him about Dora.

'Oh, Mr David, I'm very pleased!' Uriah said. 'I'll tell my mother.'

'But Agnes won't marry *you*, Uriah,' I said. I knew now that Mrs Heep was protecting her son's interests.

Uriah looked at me with his red eyes and rubbed his thin hands together again. 'Won't she, Mr David?' he said very quietly.

'No!' I said.

Later that night Mrs Heep left Agnes and me alone for a time. Mr Wickfield, Uriah and I ate dinner together. Uriah was excited. 'Have some more wine, Mr Wickfield!' he suggested. Mr Wickfield drank a lot and became quite drunk. Uriah did not drink much, but he seemed very happy.

'Agnes is a beautiful girl!' he said. Mr Wickfield put his glass down. 'Her husband will be a lucky man!' Uriah continued.

'Husband!' Mr Wickfield said. 'Husband?'

'Yes, I said "husband",' Uriah said. 'I want to marry her.'

'You? Her husband? You dog!'

Mr Wickfield stood up and his face was white and angry. His glass dropped to the floor and broke. 'You!' he shouted. 'You? *Her* husband? You dog!'

Then Uriah was angry, too. 'Don't say that, Wickfield!' he shouted. 'I own you! Remember that! I *can* marry your daughter if I want to!'

Mr Wickfield moved round the table towards Uriah. 'You – you–' he began.

At that moment Agnes came quickly into the room. 'I heard your voices,' she said. 'Come with me, Father. Come to bed.' She took Mr Wickfield away.

'He's drunk,' Uriah said to me. 'Tomorrow he'll be sorry. Forget this, Mr David.'

'I will,' I said. I was very angry with Uriah. 'Good night!' I left Uriah alone.

The next morning I had to leave Canterbury. Uriah was being quite friendly to Mr Wickfield, but Mr Wickfield was very quiet. I saw Agnes for a few minutes.

'Goodbye, Agnes,' I said. I shook her hand. 'Marry a *good* man, Agnes.'

'Yes, David,' she said. 'Don't worry.' But her face was sad.

I arrived in London and told my aunt about Uriah. She was angry too.

'Agnes *can't* marry Uriah,' my aunt agreed. 'I hate that man.'

One day I was walking home from work when I saw a man outside a church. I went up to him and took his hand. 'Mr Peggotty!' I cried. 'This is a surprise. How are you?'

'I'm well, thank you, Mr David,' Mr Peggotty said.

'And Emily?' I asked.

Mr Peggotty shook his head. 'There's no news of her,' he said.

'Where have you been?' I asked.

'I've been to France,' Mr Peggotty said. 'I can't speak French, but the people were very kind to me. I walked and walked, looking for Emily. But I didn't find her. So I came back to England and went to Yarmouth. There was a letter from Emily and some money at my house. The letter asked me to forgive her, but Emily didn't sign the letter. Here's the money.' Mr Peggotty showed me a fifty-pound note.

A woman was standing near us. I looked at her but she did not go away. I knew her from Yarmouth; it was Martha Endells.

'How is Ham?' I asked.

'He's well, too, Mr David,' said Mr Peggotty. 'He works hard but he's very unhappy.'

'What will you do now?' I asked.

'I'll look for Emily,' he said. 'I have to go now. Goodbye, Mr David.' Mr Peggotty shook my hand and I watched him. He walked down the street and he did not look back.

I could not see Martha Endells now. I walked on, feeling sad for Mr Peggotty and sorry for Emily too.

Dora's aunts wrote a reply to my letter. 'You can come to our house and visit Dora,' the letter said. 'Please bring a friend with you.'

I took Traddles with me. He talked to me about Sophy. 'Sophy is a dear girl,' he said. 'I love her very much and I want to marry her soon. But her sisters want her to stay at home and look after them. They don't like me at all.'

'But Sophy wants to marry you, doesn't she?' I asked.

'Oh, yes,' Traddles said. His face was sad. 'But when I ask Sophy about a date for the wedding, she can't tell me. I don't feel very confident about it.'

'Don't worry, Traddles,' I said. 'You *will* marry Sophy. You can wait.'

'Yes,' Traddles said. 'Sophy and I are young. We can wait.'

Dora's aunts were quite old. Their names were Miss Lavinia and Miss Clarissa. They wore black clothes and their voices were calm and quiet. They talked to us politely. At the end of the visit

Miss Clarissa said, 'You can come here twice a week on Saturdays and Sundays. Will you like that?'

'Oh, yes, Miss Clarissa,' I said. 'Thank you very much.'

So I visited Dora every week. My aunt came with me sometimes. She liked Dora and her aunts very much. Everyone was very kind to Dora – almost too kind. She did not have to do anything for herself. I did not like this; Dora needed an education.

'Dora, my dear,' I said to her one day.

'Yes, David,' Dora said.

'I have bought a book for you.'

'Oh, thank you, David!' she cried.

'It's a cookbook,' I said.

'Oh!' Dora was less excited now. 'A cookbook!'

'Read it,' I said. 'You'll learn a lot about cooking.'

'I'll try,' Dora agreed. She sounded sad.

She tried for a time but she soon stopped. 'I don't like cooking, David,' she told me. 'It's very difficult.'

When Agnes visited London, she met Dora. She liked her very much. After her visit, Dora asked me about Agnes.

'She's very pretty, isn't she?' Dora said.

'Yes, she's quite pretty,' I said.

'You knew her when you were a child, didn't you?' Dora asked. 'And you liked her then?'

I agreed that Agnes was a very good friend then. And I liked her very much now, too.

'So why do you love *me*?' Dora asked.

'Agnes is like my sister,' I said. 'And I love *you* like a wife.'

Chapter 13   I Get Married

I worked very hard. I earned money using my shorthand. I wrote a short story and was given money for that. Excited by my success, I began to write more stories. The months went past and I was twenty-one. I was a man at last! Now, I thought, Dora and I could marry.

I found a nice little house. 'We'll get it ready together,' I told Dora. 'We need to buy furniture.'

We went to the shops often but we did not buy much. 'Tables and chairs don't really interest me,' Dora said. She did buy a little house for Jip, though. It had bells on it. 'That's pretty!' Dora cried. 'Jip will like that!'

I was unhappy. I wanted to buy things for our new home. We did not have the money for things that were not necessary. But I loved Dora so I did not complain.

Then our wedding day arrived. Traddles took me to the church. Sophy and Agnes were there with Dora. Dora was very excited, and Agnes was kind to her. My aunt and Dora's aunts sat in the church and cried.

I do not remember the service very well. There was a wedding breakfast later but I do not remember that either. I was so happy and the day was like a dream.

Then the carriage took Dora and me to our new home. At last we were alone. We went inside together and closed the door.

'Are you happy, David?' Dora asked. I put my arms around her and looked into her beautiful blue eyes.

'Happy, my dear?' I said. 'Oh, yes! This is the happiest day of my life.'

'I'm really your wife now,' Dora said. 'You aren't sorry, are you?'

'No,' I said. 'How can I be sorry?'

My married life began and I continued to love Dora. But she

was not able to manage the home. We had a number of different servants, one after another. The first girl, Mary Ann, was unintelligent and drank too much.

'Dora,' I complained one evening, 'dinner is late. It was late last night. Dinner is always late in this house and Mary Ann is a terrible cook. You should speak to her about it!'

'Oh, David, I can't,' Dora said. 'I can't give her orders – I'm afraid of her.' And she began to cry.

'Don't cry, please,' I said. 'I'm sorry. I will speak to Mary Ann.'

I spoke to Mary Ann and sent her away. Then we had a woman who was too old to work. She was useless in the house, so I sent her away too. Dora employed a number of servants and they were all bad.

She also spent money without thinking, so we never had enough. Often we were unable to pay our bills. I talked to her and she cried again.

'Oh, David,' she said. 'I'm a bad wife. I'm not clever and I can't manage servants or save money. But you married me and now you're sorry. I'm very sorry, too. I love you, David.' When she looked at me, her beautiful eyes were full of tears.

'Don't be sorry, Dora, my dear,' I said. 'Don't cry. Dry your tears. *I'm* not sorry. You are my wife and I love you.'

This made Dora happy again. I did not discuss money with her after that, but I talked to my aunt.

'Can you help us, Aunt Betsey?' I asked. 'Teach Dora about money, please.'

My aunt refused. 'No, I won't do that. Remember your mother, David. She was like Dora, just a child. She was afraid of me, because I spoke unkindly to her. I don't want to make Dora afraid of me. She loves you very much, David – don't forget that. She is not clever; she is kind and pretty, though, and she loves you. That's enough. Don't be angry with her.'

'I won't, Aunt Betsey,' I agreed. I knew that she was right.

Traddles came to dinner once. The food was terrible. The servant dropped the plates and Jip walked on the table. I was angry, but Traddles only laughed. He told us stories and seemed quite happy.

When he went home, Dora came to me with her finger in her mouth. She looked very sad.

'David,' she said. 'Everything went wrong. I know that you felt very uncomfortable. I'm sorry.'

'Don't worry about it, Dora, my dear,' I said.

'But I *am* worried,' Dora said. 'I want to be a good wife but I can't be. I'm not clever. I try very hard but I can't turn this house into a home. Don't be angry. Please don't be angry with me.'

I was not angry with her, but she was no help to me at home or at work. But when I wrote stories at night, she sat by my chair; she watched me working, and I liked that.

One day Rosa Dartle sent for me, so I hurried to Mrs Steerforth's house. There Rosa gave me some surprising news. I went to the place where Mr Peggotty was staying. He was sitting in his room.

'Emily has left Steerforth!' I told him.

'Has she?' He stood up quickly. 'My poor little Emily! Where is she?'

'I don't know,' I said.

'She isn't dead!' Mr Peggotty said. 'My Emily isn't dead! I was living in fear and now I can hope again! How can we find her?'

'She won't go home to Yarmouth,' I said. 'She won't want to face people that she knows. Perhaps she will come to London, where she can hide in the crowds.'

'Yes, she can hide here,' Mr Peggotty said.

'But we can find her,' I said. 'Do you remember Martha Endells?'

'Yes, I do,' Mr Peggotty said. 'Emily helped her once.'

'Martha is in London,' I said. 'Perhaps she can help Emily now.'

We walked the streets, looking for Martha. After a time we saw her. Her clothes were old and dirty and her face was very sad. We did not speak to her but we followed her. We wanted to know where she was living.

She walked through a very poor area of town, through dirty, narrow streets. When she reached the river, she stopped. She did not see us behind her. It was a rainy night and we watched her look down at the cold, dark river.

'Martha!' I shouted. I ran to her and I took her arm. She began to cry. 'Oh, the river! The river!' she said. 'Let me go! I want to die. I have nothing to live for. Let me die!'

'Take her arm, Mr Peggotty,' I said. Mr Peggotty took Martha's arm and we pulled her away from the river. Martha cried loudly and she could not speak.

'Be calm, Martha,' I said. 'We will help you. Will you help us?'

Finally Martha was quiet. 'Who are you and what do you want?' she asked me.

I told her about Emily. Martha looked at me. 'I remember you now,' she said. She dried her tears. 'Emily was a good friend to me,' she said. 'She helped me once and now I will help her. I will ask people about her. I'll find her and take her to my room. Then I'll come and tell you the news. You saved my life tonight.'

'Thank you, Martha,' I said. 'Let us give you some money.'

'No,' Martha said, shaking her head. 'I don't want money. But what is your address?'

I gave her my address. Then I left Mr Peggotty and went home.

'Let me go! I want to die. I have nothing to live for.'

Chapter 14 I Discover a Secret

I finished my first book. It sold well and I earned a lot of money from it. We had more to spend now, but the problems at home continued. Dora could not manage the house; servants came and went. One was a boy, who stole money from us. He went to prison.

'Dora, my dear,' I said to her after that, 'things are not going well.'

'What do you mean?' she asked.

'We can't continue like this,' I explained. 'We have to employ better servants.'

'It's me,' Dora said, with tears in her eyes. 'Oh, David, I try but I can't choose servants. I don't know what to say to them.'

'Don't worry, Dora,' I said, kissing her. 'I'll manage the servants now.' Our home life got better, but my life became more difficult. I worked hard at my job and I worked hard in the house too.

'Dora has to change,' I thought to myself one day. 'At the moment she's a child, not a wife. I'll talk to her and I'll read books to her. Then perhaps she'll learn something about life.'

So I tried to teach Dora and I read books to her. But she was not interested and she learnt very little.

'We'll have a baby,' I thought. 'Perhaps Dora will make a good mother. That will give her an interest in life.'

We had a baby but sadly it died. Dora was very ill after that and stayed in bed all day. Then, when she felt a little better, my aunt spent a lot of time with her. They talked and laughed happily.

'David,' Dora said to me one day. It was some time after the baby's death. 'You're not unhappy, are you?'

'Unhappy?' I said. 'No, my dear.'

'I'm not a good wife,' Dora said. 'I know that. I can't manage the house and I don't really understand your books. But I love you, David. I love you very much. You *do* really love me, don't you?'

'Oh, yes, Dora,' I said. 'I love you. I'll always love you.'

I loved Dora very much but my life felt dull and empty. Dora could not be a large part of it. I was more like a father than a husband to her. This continued to worry me.

One day Mr Micawber wrote me a strange letter. He needed my help, he said; he had a terrible secret and he could not tell his wife about it.

I told Traddles about the letter. When I invited Mr Micawber to my house, he was there too. Mr Micawber came looking pale and sad.

'How are you, Mr Micawber?' I asked. 'And how is Mr Wickfield?'

'He's well, thank you,' Mr Micawber said. 'He's growing old but he's well.'

'And Uriah Heep – is *he* well?' Traddles asked.

Mr Micawber could not speak for a moment. His face changed colour, from red to white. Then he shouted, 'Heep! Uriah Heep! He's a dog! An animal!'

'Please be calm, Mr Micawber,' I said. 'We won't talk about him. How is Miss Wickfield?'

'Miss Wickfield?' he said and his voice changed. 'She's well. She's sweet and kind – I can't think about Miss Wickfield –I–' And Mr Micawber began to cry.

I looked at Traddles and he looked at me. We were both surprised. Mr Micawber was acting very strangely and we did not understand the problem. He began to speak again.

'I can't do it!' he cried. 'You're all kind to me, but you don't know. I'm as bad as Heep. But I'll tell you everything – all about Heep! I'll probably go to prison and my family will be poor again. It doesn't matter – I can't go on like this!'

Mr Micawber was shouting and crying now and we understood nothing.

'Be calm, Mr Micawber,' I said. 'Sit down and please be calm!'

'No!' he shouted. 'I can't be calm! I hate him! Come to Canterbury and I will tell you Heep's secrets! Come next week!' Mr Micawber stopped and looked at us. Then he ran out of the house.

'Oh, dear!' Traddles said. 'This is bad! Is Mr Micawber crazy?'

But Mr Micawber was clearly not crazy. He sent us a letter. He asked us to forgive him. He also repeated his invitation. He wanted us to come to Canterbury and he wanted to tell us about Heep.

The following evening I was walking in my garden. I was thinking about Mr Micawber's secret. A woman came in through the gate. 'Mr Copperfield!' she said.

'Martha!' I answered. 'Have you any news?'

'Yes,' she said. 'But where is Mr Peggotty? I've got to find him.'

'He often visits me here,' I said. 'But he isn't here tonight.'

'I've been to his room,' she said. 'He isn't there. I have left a letter for him. Please come with me!'

Martha took me to a poor house. We went upstairs. There was a woman on the stairs in front of us.

'I know that woman!' I said quietly. 'It's—'

'Don't speak!' Martha said.

We followed the woman. She stopped outside a door and looked at the name on it. Then she went inside.

'Let's go in!' I said. 'Is Emily there? We have to help her. That woman is Rosa Dartle.'

'Wait!' Martha said. 'Wait and listen.'

We listened outside the door.

'Your name is Emily, isn't it?' Rosa asked.

'Yes,' Emily said. 'But who – who are you?'

'My name is Rosa Dartle,' she said. 'I live with Mrs Steerforth.'

'Steerforth!' Emily said in a low voice.

'Yes. Steerforth,' Rosa said. Her voice was cold and hard. 'Let me look at you. Yes, a pretty, stupid face and a bad heart! I know.'

'No!' Emily began to cry. 'Why have you come here? Why do you say these terrible things?'

'I hate you!' Rosa said. 'You took Steerforth away from his mother – and from *me*! I hate you. Your pretty face deceived him. You wanted his money, so you took him away from us.'

'No,' Emily cried. 'I loved him. At first he loved me too.'

'Love?' Rosa said. '*You* can't love. You're not a lady. You're a fisherman's daughter. Steerforth *bought* you. You wanted money and he bought you.'

'No! It isn't true!' Emily said. 'Why are you here?'

'I want to hurt you,' Rosa said. 'You hurt me and now I'm going to hurt you. Leave this house and go back to your family!'

'I can't! Oh, I can't!' Emily cried. 'I want to see my family and my Uncle Peggotty again but I can't.'

'Then leave England,' Rosa ordered. 'I'll drive you away. I'll tell people about you and they'll hate you, too. Go away!'

'Don't be cruel!' Emily cried. 'Let me stay. I'm not really a bad woman. Please let me stay!'

'No!' Rosa shouted. 'Go! I hate you!'

Rosa hurried out of the room. She did not see Martha and me in the darkness. She passed a man on the stairs without seeing him. It was Mr Peggotty. He was holding Martha's letter and he went into Emily's room. We could hear her crying.

'Emily, my dear!' we heard. 'At last I've found you! Thank God! Don't cry, my dear. Now you're safe.'

'I won't stay here,' I told Martha. 'If Emily sees me, she'll feel worse. Mr Peggotty will come to my house and tell me about her. Thank you, Martha.' I left her and went home.

That night Mr Peggotty came. Dora was upstairs in bed. He told me all about Emily. 'I'm very happy,' he said. 'I've found her at last. She's had a terrible time but she's more cheerful now. Last night she told me everything. When she came back to England, she met Martha. Martha saved her. She took Emily to her room and looked after her.'

'What will you do now?' I asked.

'Emily can't live in Yarmouth,' he said. 'The people there know her well and they know her story. It will be too difficult for her. So we'll go away. We'll leave England and move to Australia. But we can't go for a few weeks. I need to give Mrs Gummidge some money and find a house for her. Then we'll leave.'

At that time Peggotty, my old servant, was living in Ham's house and looking after Ham.

'Your sister will be sorry,' I said. 'She won't go to Australia with you, will she?'

'No, I don't think so,' Mr Peggotty replied sadly. 'Mr David,' he went on, 'I have a letter here for Mrs Steerforth. I'm sending her the money that Steerforth gave Emily. Will you take it to her?'

'Yes,' I promised. 'I will.'

'And will you come to Yarmouth with me and see my sister? That will make her happy.'

'Yes, of course I will.'

So I went to Yarmouth with Mr Peggotty.

I saw Peggotty and then I went for a walk with Ham. 'Mr Copperfield,' he said. 'You'll see Emily. She knows that I forgive her. I love her but I can't see her. She needs a happier life now. I don't want her to think of me and of the past.' Ham put his strong hand on my arm. 'So tell her this, Mr Copperfield. Say to her, "Emily, don't be sorry about Ham. He is happy. He has a happy life." Then she'll be happy too.'

Ham was a good man. I shook his hand. Then I left him and went to Mr Peggotty's house. Emily was in bed, and Mrs Gummidge was sitting with Mr Peggotty.

'Oh, Mr Copperfield,' Mrs Gummidge said. 'Tell him! Tell Mr

Peggotty that he mustn't leave me in England!' She took Mr Peggotty's arm. 'Let me come with you, Daniel,' she said. 'Let me be part of your new life in Australia. Don't leave me here!'

'I won't leave you, Mrs Gummidge,' Mr Peggotty agreed. 'You can come too.'

'Oh, thank you, Daniel, thank you!' she said. 'I *won't* be sad and I won't complain. I'll work hard for you and Emily.'

The next day I left Yarmouth and returned to London. There I met Traddles – it was time to see Mr Micawber. My aunt went with us to Canterbury, where we visited Mr Wickfield's office. Mr Wickfield was ill in bed, and Mr Micawber took us to Uriah Heep.

'This *is* nice!' Uriah said. 'Mr Copperfield! And Miss Trotwood! And Mr Traddles!' He rubbed his hands together and he smiled. But it was not a friendly smile. 'Mr Micawber, you can go,' he ordered.

'I won't go,' Mr Micawber said quickly. He was holding a letter in his hand.

'Oh! I understand!' Uriah said. 'You are all against me! Copperfield, I know that you hate me. Now you have made my servant, Micawber, hate me too!'

'*You* are the one who makes trouble, Heep!' Mr Micawber cried. 'You have done terrible things to Mr Wickfield. Listen! I have written it all down in this letter.'

'Give me that letter!' Uriah shouted. He tried to take the letter but Mr Micawber hit him across the face. Uriah shouted with surprise and pain and jumped back. Mrs Heep ran into the room.

'Be quiet, Heep!' Mr Micawber cried. 'I *will* read my letter!'

'Oh, be humble, Uriah!' Mrs Heep said. 'Be nice to these people.'

'No, mother,' Uriah said angrily. 'But let him read his letter. I'm not afraid of anyone.'

Mr Micawber began to read. 'I came and worked for Heep,' he

'Give me that letter!'

said. 'You all know that. I borrowed money from him and I could not pay it back. So Heep ordered me to work for him. I had to choose between helping him and prison, so I took the job. I have helped Heep to steal from Mr Wickfield. People give Mr Wickfield their money to look after, and then Heep steals it. He tells Mr Wickfield that Mr Wickfield has stolen it; that he has signed the papers while he is drunk. Mr Wickfield believes him and has become sick with worry.'

'Prove it, Micawber!' Uriah shouted. 'You can't prove it!'

'I *can* prove it!' Mr Micawber said. 'I have the papers. I took them from your desk. You wrote everything down in a little book. *I* have that book!'

'Oh, be humble, Uriah!' Mrs Heep cried.

'Be quiet, mother!' Uriah shouted. 'Go on,' he told Mr Micawber. Mr Micawber read from his letter again. 'Heep also stole money that belonged to Mr Wickfield. But Mr Wickfield is afraid of Heep, so he has not told anyone. Heep has stolen a lot of money and I can prove it!'

'My money!' my aunt shouted. She jumped at Heep. She held him and shook him. '*You* stole my money. I thought that Mr Wickfield was managing my money badly. So I did not tell Agnes that he lost it. But *you* stole the money. Now I can speak. Give me my money!'

'Don't hurt him, Aunt,' I said, and pulled her away.

'What will you do now, Heep?' Traddles asked. 'Do we have to send you to prison?'

'Prison? Oh, my poor Uriah!' Mrs Heep cried.

'Be quiet, Mother!' Uriah said. He looked at us all with his little red eyes. 'No,' he said. 'I won't go to prison. I will pay the money back.' He left the room angrily.

'Oh, I'm a happy man now!' Mr Micawber said. 'I was as dishonest as Heep. But now I've told you and I can talk to my family again. I don't have any secrets. I'm a happy man!'

'Now you have no job, Mr Micawber,' my aunt said. 'What will you do?'

'A job?' Mr Micawber said. 'I can't think about jobs now. Perhaps we will all go to Australia. Oh, I'm a happy man! I'm going to see my family!' And Mr Micawber ran, singing, out of the room.

I looked at my aunt and my aunt looked at me. We both laughed.

Chapter 15   I Lose Many Good Friends

Now my story becomes very sad. Dora's illness got worse and she was unable to leave her bed. She continued to play with Jip, who stayed with her night and day. Jip was growing old and could not run around.

'Jip's old, Dora,' my aunt said. 'Can I buy a young dog for you? A young dog will be more fun for you.'

'Oh, no, thank you, Aunt Betsey,' Dora said. 'When I look at Jip, I remember happier days. David brought me flowers once and Jip bit them in half. I don't want another dog.'

Poor Jip was old and slow and Dora was pale and ill. But she always smiled when I sat with her. We talked happily for hours.

One day there was no smile on her poor, white face. 'David,' she said. 'I want Agnes. Please ask her to come.'

So I wrote to Agnes, who came quickly. She sat next to Dora's bed and she talked to her. Her calmness and kindness always helped Dora.

The days passed and Dora grew very quiet. She could not sit up in bed now, and her voice was very soft.

One night Agnes came to me looking very unhappy. 'Dora wants you,' Agnes said, and I hurried upstairs. Dora looked very small in the big bed but her face was as pretty as ever.

'Sit down, David, my dear,' Dora said quietly. I sat next to her and I held her hand.

'David,' she said. 'I have been a bad wife, but I always loved you. Forgive me.'

'Oh, Dora, my dear,' I said, and I was crying. 'You weren't a bad wife. I love you very much.'

'Thank you,' Dora answered quietly. 'I'm leaving you now. I'm sorry, my dear, but I'm happy too. Now you can find someone who will be a good wife to you.'

'Oh, no!' I cried. 'I don't want a new wife, Dora! I want *you!*'

Dora touched my hair. 'Thank you,' she said. 'You are kind to want your poor, stupid Dora. Now kiss me, David, and then send Agnes to me again.'

I kissed Dora and then I went downstairs to find Agnes. Jip followed me down and lay near my chair.

'Oh, Jip!' I said. 'Poor Dora! Perhaps she's dying! Then you'll be very sad. Poor Jip!'

But Jip was not moving. I touched him. Poor Jip was dead.

At that moment, Agnes came into the room. I looked at her face and I knew. 'Agnes!' I cried. I jumped out of my chair. 'Dora – Tell me! Is she–?'

'She's dead, David,' Agnes said very quietly.

I do not remember that time well. I stopped talking to people and I spent a lot of time in tears.

'I will leave England,' I thought. 'England is a very sad place for me, now. There are too many memories. But first I should see Mr Micawber and Traddles.'

They were both in Canterbury helping Mr Wickfield. 'Thanks to Uriah Heep, Mr Wickfield has lost a lot of money,' Traddles told me. 'It's gone, so he's quite poor now. He's ill, too. But Agnes will help him. She's going to start a little school to make money. But we have found five thousand pounds of Miss Trotwood's money. She'll be able to live comfortably on that.'

'She's dead, David,' Agnes said very quietly.

I told my aunt about the money. 'I'll help the Micawbers,' said my aunt. 'Mr Micawber owes money to Uriah Heep and he can't pay. If I pay the money back, he won't go to prison.'

We went to Mr Micawber's house. All the Micawbers were wearing new clothes for Australia. They looked rather strange, but Mr Micawber was proud of them.

'I'm a happy man!' he said. 'There are no more secrets and I'm going to Australia soon. I'll be an important man in Australia!' And Mr Micawber laughed.

A man came to the door. 'Mr Micawber?' he asked.

'Yes,' said Mr Micawber. 'I'm Micawber.'

'Then I'm taking you to prison,' the man said. 'You owe Mr Heep twenty pounds. This paper proves it.'

'No! Oh, no!' Mr Micawber shouted. 'I haven't any money! I don't want to go to prison! I'll die in prison! My family will die, too. They haven't any money. Oh, I'm a very unhappy man!' And Mr Micawber cried.

'Don't worry, Mr Micawber,' my aunt said. 'This is the reason why I came. Here is the twenty pounds.' I paid the man and he went away.

Mr Micawber kissed my aunt's hand. 'You *are* good!' he said. 'I'm saved again. Thank you.' He sang a little song and made drinks for us.

That night my aunt talked about Mr Micawber. 'Mr Micawber needs more money for Australia,' she said. 'I will give him five hundred pounds.'

'Don't give the money to Mr Micawber,' I told her. 'It isn't safe with him. Mr Peggotty is going to Australia, too. Give the money to him. He can keep the money for Mr Micawber and look after it.'

'That's a good idea,' my aunt agreed. 'I'll do that.'

'I'll visit Mr Peggotty and talk to him,' I said.

I went to see Mr Peggotty in London and told him about Mr

Micawber and about my aunt's money.

'I'll help Mr Micawber,' Mr Peggotty said. 'I'll look after his money for him.'

'Thank you,' I said.

'Emily has written Ham a letter,' Mr Peggotty said. 'I can't take it to him because I'm very busy. What do you suggest?'

'I'm not busy,' I said. I was happy to do things for him. I wanted to be busy, and not to think about Dora. 'I'll go to Yarmouth and take the letter to Ham.'

So I took the coach to Yarmouth. It was a cold day. The sky was grey and the wind was strong and noisy. In Yarmouth it was difficult to stand up, so I went quickly to my hotel.

'This is a terrible storm, sir,' the man at the desk said to me. 'The sea is very rough. A lot of ships went down last night. A lot of men have died.'

'That *is* bad,' I said. I went to my room and waited. I wanted to find Ham and give him the letter, but the storm frightened me. In the end, I stayed in the hotel. But I could not eat my dinner and later I could not sleep. The wind shook the windows of my room. 'It's going to damage this hotel,' I thought.

The next morning I heard the sound of shouting outside. 'Quickly!' a voice shouted. 'Come quickly to the sea. A ship is going down, but perhaps we can save some men.'

I ran to the beach, fighting against the strong wind.

A large group of men were standing there. One of them was Ham.

'Where is the ship?' I shouted. It was difficult to hear anyone.

'There!'

I saw the ship. It was not far away. We could see four men at first. Then the sea came up and took two of them. Now there were only two men on the ship. One was tall and he was wearing a red hat.

'Give me a rope!' Ham shouted. 'Perhaps I can save them. I

will swim to them with the rope.'

A man brought a long rope for Ham, who tied it round his body. We all watched the ship. It was moving up and down on the stormy sea.

'Don't go, Ham!' I shouted. 'The sea will kill you! It's very strong.'

'I have to go!' Ham shouted. 'Those men need help.' He went into the sea while some of the men on the beach held the end of the rope. I watched the ship. The sea came up and covered it. Then it fell again. Now there was only one man fighting for his life. The men pulled on the rope and brought Ham back to the beach.

'You're crazy,' they said. 'You can't help him. You'll die!'

'Give me more rope!' he shouted. 'I'm going to try again. I *have* to.'

The wind was very strong. It was hurting my eyes but I could see Ham's head. He was swimming slowly to the ship. The man on the ship took off his red hat and waved it. Now Ham was near the ship and reaching out his hand to the man.

But a great sea, a mountain of water, fell on the ship. We waited and watched. The ship was gone.

'Pull the rope!' a man shouted. Pulling together, they brought Ham back to the beach. But he was dead.

'Sir!' another man called from a different part of the beach. 'Come here, quickly! I have found a body! It is a man – the man from the ship!'

There was a red hat on the sand near the dead man. I knew him. I knew him well!

'Steerforth!' I said. Tears came into my eyes. 'My wife is dead,' I said. 'Ham is dead, and now you are dead. Once you were my good friend. Poor Steerforth! And poor Ham!'

The bodies were carried away. I could not help, so I stayed on the beach. I felt very sad.

There was a red hat on the sand near the dead man.

I left Yarmouth and I returned to London. I went to Highgate and I stood outside Mrs Steerforth's house for a few minutes. The house looked dark and cold. Then I went to the door. A servant took me to Mrs Steerforth. Rosa Dartle was with her.

'Mr Copperfield!' Mrs Steerforth said. 'Why–?'

'Your son, Steerforth–' I said, and then I stopped. I could not tell them.

'Is he ill?' Mrs Steerforth said. The two women looked at me. Their faces were pale and frightened.

'Tell us!' Rosa said. 'He's dead, isn't he?'

'Yes,' I said. I told them about the storm and the ship.

Mrs Steerforth made a little sound but she did not speak. Rosa touched her scar and turned angrily to Mrs Steerforth.

'Dead!' Rosa said. 'Steerforth is dead! *You* have done this! You, his mother! You gave him too much. You were proud, so he was proud. You were both better than everyone. He gave me this scar when he was a boy. It made me ugly and changed my life. But you never spoke to him about it. You taught him to think about himself – never other people, only himself. You did that! You!'

Mrs Steerforth said nothing. She looked very old.

'Miss Dartle!' I said. 'Please stop! You are making Mrs Steerforth ill!'

'I loved him!' Rosa Dartle said. 'He was cruel to me but I loved him. I understood him. He was a proud man but I loved him. "He will love me, too," I thought. "He will marry me. He will not be a kind husband but I will be happy." But he left me. You did that! You, his mother!'

'Miss Dartle!' I said. 'Stop! Mrs Steerforth is very ill! She can't hear you!'

Rosa Dartle turned to me. 'You!' she said. 'Copperfield, his friend! What kind of friend were you to him? You took him to Yarmouth. He met Emily there, and she stole him from me. You always bring bad news! Go away! I hate you! Go!'

I stopped in the doorway and looked back. Rosa was standing next to Mrs Steerforth. She put her arms round the old woman. Mrs Steerforth did not move and Rosa began to cry. 'Oh, my dear!' she said. 'I'm sorry. I loved him but you loved him, too. Now he's dead. Poor Mrs Steerforth! Poor Steerforth!'

I left the house of tears and went home.

The Micawbers and Mr Peggotty were leaving the next day. My aunt and I went to see them on the boat.

Mr Micawber was happy again. He smiled and sang.

'I'll work hard in Australia,' he promised my aunt. 'I'll be a success.' He kissed her hand. 'Thank you, Miss Trotwood!'

Mr Peggotty came up to me. 'Did Ham get the letter?' he asked.

'Yes,' I said. This was not true. Ham was dead. But I could not tell Mr Peggotty in his happiness. 'Where's Emily?' I asked.

'There,' he said, and I saw two women sitting together, Emily and Martha. 'Martha wants to come with us,' Mr Peggotty said. 'She can start a new life in Australia. We'll all have a new and better life.'

'Goodbye, Mr Peggotty,' I said. 'Say goodbye to Emily and Martha for me.'

'I will,' Mr Peggotty said. 'And I'll come back. I'll see you again, Mr David.' He shook my hand.

I went back to the Micawbers. Mrs Micawber held my hand and cried.

'I'll write letters from Australia, my dear Copperfield,' Mr Micawber said. 'Goodbye!'

'Goodbye,' I said. 'Good luck!'

'We're sailing now!' a man shouted. My aunt and I left the ship and watched from the land. The ropes were untied and fell into the water. The ship began to move away. My aunt and I shouted goodbye. Mr Peggotty and the Micawbers shouted back.

'They're all beginning a new life,' my aunt said. I felt very sad.

These were my friends and they were leaving me. My wife, Steerforth and Ham were all dead.

'I need to begin a new life too,' I said. 'I'll go abroad and travel for a few months. Then, perhaps, I'll learn to forget.'

Chapter 16　I Find Complete Happiness

I visited very many countries, but I did not forget. I often thought about poor Ham and proud Steerforth. My heart was full of my love for Dora, but she was not with me. My life was empty and I wanted to die too.

I fell ill and could not work. The months passed and I discovered Switzerland. I lived there in the mountains and slowly started to forget. When I was well, I began to meet people. I was interested in life again.

I wrote a new book, which I sent to Traddles. He sold it for me, and I earned enough money to live on.

One day I received a letter from Agnes. It was a kind, happy letter and I read it many times. While I was reading it, a new thought came to me. I loved her and wanted to marry her. But to her I was just a brother; she did not want to be my wife. I decided, though, to return to England.

I went to London. It was very cold but I was happy to see the streets and houses again. I went to Traddles's house first. He was living in three small rooms. While I was walking up the stairs, I could hear girls' voices. 'That's strange,' I thought. 'Who are they?'

Traddles opened the door. 'Copperfield!' he shouted. 'Come in! Come in! You look well!'

'My dear old friend,' I said and shook his hand. Then I saw that he was not alone.

'This is Sophy, my wife,' Traddles said. 'I'm a happy man, Copperfield! I'm married. Married!'

'You didn't tell me!' I cried.

'No,' Traddles laughed. 'It's a surprise!'

Sophy was a very pretty girl and clearly a good wife. Her four sisters were living there too, in quite a small space. But Sophy managed the home very well and looked after all of them. The rooms were comfortable and Traddles was happy. I talked to them all and we laughed a lot together. I enjoyed my first evening in London very much.

The next morning I went to Dover to see my aunt. She told me all the news. Both Mr Peggotty and Mr Micawber were happy in Australia. Mr Micawber was working hard and he was not borrowing money. He sent my aunt money when he could.

'And Agnes? Is she married?' I asked.

'No,' said my aunt. 'But it's possible that she will marry soon.'

'Oh!' I cried.

My aunt looked at me strangely. 'Agnes is a pretty girl with a very warm heart,' she said. 'A lot of men want to marry her.'

'I know that,' I said.

'She isn't silly,' my aunt continued. 'Some girls are silly.' She looked hard at me again. 'Some *men* are silly.'

I left my aunt in Dover and went next to Canterbury. Mr Wickfield was not at home, so Agnes was alone.

'Hello, David,' she said. 'How are you?'

'I'm very well,' I said. 'I'm well and happy.' This was not true. I was not happy, but I could not tell Agnes that. 'You have some good news for me, haven't you?' I asked.

'Good news?' Agnes asked. 'I don't understand.'

'You're going to get married. Isn't that good news?'

'No,' Agnes replied. 'It isn't true. I won't marry. I can't marry.' Suddenly tears came into her eyes. 'Oh, I'm being silly,' she said. 'Don't look at me.'

'My dear!' I said. 'What is wrong? Why can't you marry?'

'I love a man,' she said. 'But I can't marry him because he

doesn't love me. I loved him as a child and now I love him as a woman.'

'Really?' I said. 'Agnes! Who is the man?' Agnes turned away. 'I can't tell you,' she said.

I held her arms. 'Agnes!' I ordered. 'Tell me! Who is the man?'

Agnes looked into my eyes. 'You are the man, David,' she said. 'I'm sorry. You feel like a brother and not like a husband to me. I know that.'

'But I want to be your husband!' I cried. 'I love you Agnes. I didn't understand my feelings, but now I do. I love you. Will you marry me?'

'Oh, yes, David,' Agnes said. 'I *will* marry you.'

I put my arms round her and I looked into her eyes. 'Why are you sad?' I asked.

'I'm not really sad,' she said. 'But I'm thinking about Dora. I went to her room when she was dying. You remember that. She asked me to promise her something. She told me to marry you. And then she died.'

'You should keep the promise,' I said, and I kissed her.

Mr Wickfield came in, and we told him the news. He was very pleased. I went straight back to Dover and Agnes went with me.

'Hello, David,' my aunt said. 'Hello, Agnes.' She looked at us.

'You were right, Aunt,' I said. 'Agnes *is* going to marry soon.'

'Oh!' my aunt said. She looked very sad. 'Is that really true?'

'I'm afraid so.'

'Oh, dear!' my aunt said. 'Who is she going to marry?'

'Me!' I cried, and I kissed my aunt. 'She is going to marry me!'

'Oh! Oh! I'm so happy!' my aunt said. 'She always loved you, David. I know that. Oh!' My aunt was very excited. She laughed until she cried.

And so I married Agnes. We lived in London, and we had children.

One day a visitor came to the house. It was Mr Peggotty, who

I put my arms round her and I looked into her eyes.

wanted to see us and to see our children. We asked him about Emily.

'Emily did not marry,' he said. 'But she is happy. She helps people and she likes that.'

'How is Martha?' we asked.

'Martha married a young man,' Mr Peggotty said. 'He is kind to her and they are happy too.'

'And Mrs Gummidge?' Mr Peggotty shook his grey head and he laughed.

'Mrs Gummidge did not marry again,' he said. 'A man wanted to make her his wife, but she refused him. She's very cheerful these days. She works hard and she looks after me well.'

'And Mr Micawber?' we asked. 'Is he in trouble again?'

'Oh, I have good news about Mr Micawber,' Mr Peggotty told us. 'He's a successful man now. He soon earned money and became quite rich. He gave me a letter for you. Here it is.' Mr Peggotty passed me the letter. The Micawber family were all well and enjoying life in Australia.

◆

The years are passing and we have five children now. My aunt is happy because one of them is a little girl. Her name is Dora. Peggotty lives with us and looks after the children.

Traddles is a rich lawyer, who does not need to save money. He and Sophy live happily with Sophy's sisters in a fine, big house.

It is late at night and I am tired of writing. But I am happy because I am not alone. When I turn my head, I can see her. It is late but she is sitting near me and working too. When I look at her, she smiles her quiet smile. She will always be with me – my good, kind wife, my dear Agnes.

Silas Marner
George Eliot

Silas Marner leads a simple life as a weaver in the village of Raveloe. All he does is work, he has no friends and the only thing he loves is his money, which he counts every day. Then one day his money is stolen and a little girl comes to live with him. Soon Silas Marner starts to change.

Braveheart
Randall Wallace

'Sons of Scotland, you have come here to fight as free men . . . if you fight perhaps you'll die.'

Braveheart is the true story of William Wallace who led his people to fight for the country they loved.

Braveheart is an exhilarating and moving film directed by and starring Mel Gibson. It won five Oscars at the Academy Awards.

Forrest Gump
Winston Groom

"I was born an idiot – but I'm cleverer than most people think," says Forrest Gump. And this soon becomes clear in this wonderfully warm and funny story about a good-hearted young man from Alabama who wins a medal for bravery in the Vietnam War, who meets the President of the United States of America, and whose best friend is an ape called Sue! *Forrest Gump is also an Oscar-winning film, starring Tom Hanks and Sally Field.*

There are hundreds of Penguin Readers to choose from – world classics, film adaptations, modern-day crime and adventure, short stories, biographies, American classics, non-fiction, plays ...

For a complete list of all Penguin Readers titles, please contact your local Pearson Longman office or visit our website.

www.penguinreaders.com

WORD LIST

carriage (n) a passenger vehicle pulled by one or more horses

cart (n) a vehicle with two or four wheels that is pulled by a man or an animal

clerk (n) someone who works with papers in an office

coach (n) a passenger vehicle with four wheels that is pulled by horses

complain (v) to say that you are unhappy about something

cruel (adj) very unkind; very unkind actions are **cruelty**

deceive (v) to lie to someone or hide the true position

donkey (n) a grey or brown animal like a small horse with long ears

educate (v) to teach someone, usually in a school or a college

gentleman (n) a polite man who acts well towards other people

humble (adj) not proud. A humble person does not believe that he or she is better than other people.

lawyer (n) someone who is paid for help with the law

manage (v) to make the decisions about money, a business or workers, for example

owe (v) to have to pay back money that you borrowed

rope (n) something strong and thick that you tie things with

rub (v) to move your hand across something repeatedly

scar (n) the sign on your skin of an old cut

servant (n) someone who works in another person's house

shilling (n) old British money. There were twenty shillings in a pound.

shorthand (n) a quick way of writing, using signs for words

35 You are David's mother. Write a letter to your son at school. Tell him why Mr Murdstone is not a bad man. Explain why school will make him a better person.

36 Steerforth says, 'I'm not really a bad man.' Do you agree? Write about him.

37 You are Dora in Chapter 10. Write a letter to your father about your love for David. Tell him why you love him. Explain why he will be a good husband.

38 You are Mr Spenlow in Chapter 11. After David loses his money, write him a letter. Tell him why he cannot marry Dora. What will you do if he tries to see her again?

39 You are David in Chapter 14. You want to find a good servant to work for you and Dora. Write about the job for a local newspaper.

40 You work for a local newspaper in Yarmouth. Describe the storm in Chapter 15. What happened on the beach?

41 You are Mr Micawber in Australia. Write a letter to David. Tell him about your past mistakes. Describe your new life.

28 Write notes for a short speech, continuing one of these statements. Then make your speech to the class.

    a I feel sorry for Rosa Dartle because ...

    b Ham is right not to see Emily because ...

    c Mr Micawber is not a bad man because ...

    d Uriah Heep should go to prison because ...

Chapters 15–16

Before you read

29 How do you think the story will end for these people?
    David   Dora   Agnes   Steerforth   Mr Micawber

While you read

30 Do these people die (**D**), go to Australia (**A**) or get married (**M**)?

a Dora	.....	**f** Traddles	.....
b Mr Micawber	.....	**g** Agnes	.....
c Ham	.....	**h** Emily	.....
d Steerforth	.....	**i** Mrs Gummidge	.....
e Martha	...../.....		

After you read

31 'All the bad people have unhappy endings.' Do you agree? Discuss this with another student.

Writing

32 Who is the most interesting person in the story? Write about him or her for a school magazine.

33 How was life difficult for poor people, children and women in the 1800s? Write about this for a magazine. Use examples from this story.

34 You are David in Chapter 3. Write a letter to your mother from school. Describe the teachers and the other students. Do you want to go home? Why (not)?

23 In Chapter 12, who says these words? Who are they talking about?

    a 'She's very pretty, and I love her very much.'

    b 'I will always help you. . . . I'll always be your friend.'

    c 'You? Her husband? You dog!'

    d 'He works hard but he's very unhappy.'

    e 'Her sisters want her to stay at home and look after them.'

    f 'I love *you* like a wife.'

After you read

24 Who are these people angry with? Why?

    a Agnes   **d** Mr Wickfield

    b Dora   **e** Mr Peggotty

    c Mr Spenlow   **f** Miss Trotwood

25 Discuss these questions with another student.

    a What really happened to Miss Trotwood's money?

    b Why does Mr Wickfield not tell Uriah Heep to leave?

Chapters 13–14

Before you read

26 Will David and Dora be happy together? Why (not)?

While you read

27 Circle the wrong words. Write the correct words.

    a Dora saves a lot of money.   ....

    b Emily is probably hiding in Yarmouth.   ....

    c Martha almost falls off a bridge.   ....

    d David becomes a lawyer.   ....

    e Mr Micawber is friendly with Uriah Heep. ....

    f Rosa hates Steerforth.   ....

    g Mr Peggotty, Emily and Ham are going to go to Australia.   ....

    h Uriah Heep has stolen money from Mr Micawber.   ....

19 Are theses sentences right (✓) or wrong (✗)?

a Traddles is a lawyer now. .....

b Mr Micawber has a job. .....

c Mr Micawber steals money from Traddles. .....

d Rosa Dartle is worried about Steerforth. .....

e Barkis dies. .....

f Emily leaves her family for Steerforth. .....

g Steerforth plans to marry Emily. .....

h Rosa is in love with Steerforth. .....

i Dora agrees to marry David. .....

j She tells her father immediately. .....

After you read

20 Discuss these questions with another student.

a Which four people cannot get married yet? Why not?

b Who do these people write letters to? What are they about?
Mr Micawber Peggotty Emily Dora

c Which of these people do you feel most sorry for? Why?
Traddles Peggotty Ham Emily Mrs Steerforth
Mr Peggotty Steerforth

Chapters 11–12

Before you read

21 David is going to receive bad news about Mr Micawber, his aunt and Dora's father. What is the news, do you think?

While you read

22 In Chapter 11, which of these people (✓) try to help David with his problems?

a Mr Micawber .....

b Mr Spenlow .....

c Agnes .....

d Dora .....

e Traddles .....

Chapters 7–8

Before you read

14 Discuss these questions. What do you think?

    a Is David right to be afraid of Uriah Heep? Why (not)?

    b What will David do when he finishes school?

While you read

15 In which order does David see these people? Number them, 1–9.

    a Rosa Dartle   .....   **f** Traddles   .....

    b Peggotty   .....   **g** Steerforth   .....

    c Mr Micawber   .....   **h** Agnes   .....

    d Dora   .....   **i** Mrs Heep   .....

    e Emily   .....

After reading

16 Are these people friends? Why (not)?

    a Mr Micawber and Uriah Heep   **d** Agnes and Uriah Heep

    b David and Agnes   **e** Dora and Miss Murdstone

    c Emily and Ham

17 Discuss these questions with another student.

    a Why does Emily say that she is bad?

    b Why does Agnes dislike Steerforth?

    c Will Dora or Agnes be a better wife for David? Why?

Chapters 9–10

Before you read

18 Discuss these questions. Will these people be happy or unhappy? Why?

    a Peggotty and Barkis   **c** David and Dora

    b Emily and Ham

Chapters 5–6

Before you read

10 In the next chapter, somebody from David's early life will help him. Who will it be? Why will he or she help?

While you read

11 Circle the correct word.
  a David *likes / dislikes* his job.
  b David *lives / works* with Mr Micawber.
  c David *rides / walks* to Dover.
  d Miss Murdstone rides to Dover *in a cart / on a donkey*.
  e Miss Trotwood *likes / dislikes* the Murdstones.
  f Miss Trotwood is *kind / unkind* to David.
  g Mr Wickfield is a *lawyer / teacher*.
  h David *likes / dislikes* his new school.

After you read

12 Find and correct the five mistakes in this description of Mr Micawber.

Mr Micawber wears dark, old clothes and has thick, grey hair. He takes David home to meet his wife and children. He has a big house with lots of furniture. Mrs Micawber tells David that her husband is a stupid man. He never has any money. One day, Mr and Mrs Micawber are taken to prison because they have stolen money.

13 Work in groups of three or four. Discuss the people in these chapters. Agree on an order, for the men and for the women, from the best person to the worst.

The men: Mr Quinion, Mr Micawber, the young man with the cart, Mr Murdstone, Mr Wickfield, Uriah Heep

The women: Mrs Micawber, Miss Trotwood, Miss Murdstone

5 Work with another student. Have this conversation.

Student A: You are Peggotty. You think that Mr Murdstone is a bad husband and father. Tell Clara why.

Student B: You are Clara. You think that Mr Murdstone is a good husband and father. Tell Peggotty why.

Chapters 3–4

Before you read

6 Work with another student. Have this conversation.

Student A: You are a boy at David's new school. Ask David about his life and family. Is he happy to be at school?

Student B: You are David. Tell the boy at your new school about your life and answer his questions.

While you read

7 Answer these questions. Write the names.

a Who is a poor teacher? ....

b Who owns David's new school? ....

c Who comes from a rich family? ....

d Who visit David at school? ....

....

e Who has a new baby? ....

f Who die? ....

....

g Who marries Peggotty? ....

h Who will be David's employer? ....

After you read

8 How does David feel about these? Why?

a his first days at school   e his first visit home

b Mr Mell   f his second visit home

c Mr and Mrs Creakle   g his visit to Yarmouth

d Traddles and Steerforth   h Peggotty's marriage to Barkis

9 Discuss these questions with another student.

a Is Steerforth a good friend for David? Why (not)?

b Was Clara a good mother? Why (not)?

ACTIVITIES

Chapters 1–2

Before you read

1 Read the Introduction to the book. Then discuss these questions about Charles Dickens with another student.
    a What other books did he write?
    b What are his stories about?
    c Did Dickens have a sad or a happy life, do you think?
    d How old was he when he wrote *David Copperfield*?

2 Look at the Word List at the back of the book. Which are words for:
    a people?
    b vehicles?

While you read

3 Tick (✓) the people and things that David likes.

Peggotty	.....	Little Emily	.....
Mr Murdstone	.....	Miss Murdstone	.....
the sea	.....	his lessons	.....
Mr Peggotty's home	.....		

After you read

4 Who do these words describe? Find the right person on the right.
    a Clara's only friend   Miss Trotwood
    b wants to be rich   Mrs Copperfield
    c David's father's aunt   Peggotty
    d weak and childlike   Mr Murdstone
    e a kind man   Mrs Gummidge
    f angry and cruel   Little Emily
    g always unhappy   Mr Peggotty

94